Michael H. Lubetsky

TUTTLE PUBLISHING
Tokyo • Rutland, Vermont • Singapore

Table of Contents

PREFACE — 4

1 WHAT IS DEBATE? — 6
- **DEBATE FOCUS:** Debate vs Argument and Discussion
- **LANGUAGE FOCUS:** Definitions, Derivations, Using a Dictionary, Expressing Opinions, Expressing Agreement/Disagreement, Listening for Gist

2 TENNIS DEBATE — 14
- **DEBATE FOCUS:** Making and Refuting Arguments
- **LANGUAGE FOCUS:** Comparisons, Contrasts, Conditional Statements

3 RESOLUTIONS AND CASES — 22
- **DEBATE FOCUS:** Casing a Resolution
- **LANGUAGE FOCUS:** Brainstorming, Paraphrasing

4 POINTS — 30
- **DEBATE FOCUS:** Making Points, Flowing
- **LANGUAGE FOCUS:** Note-taking, Reading Back From Notes

5 THE FIRST AFFIRMATIVE CONSTRUCTIVE — 38
- **DEBATE FOCUS:** Links, Opening Speeches
- **LANGUAGE FOCUS:** Abbreviations, Longer Listening with Notetaking

6 The First Negative Constructive   46
Debate Focus:
Refutation, Opening Negative Speeches

Language Focus:
Longer Listening with Notetaking

7 Holistic Reasoning   54
Debate Focus:
Bringing Points together in a Logical Framework

Language Focus:
Contrafactual Speculation, Defining Abstract Terms

8 Members' Speeches   62
Debate Focus:
Later Speeches, Critiquing Speeches

Language Focus:
Longer Listening with Notetaking

9 Rebuttals and Adjudication   70
Debate Focus:
Closing Speeches, Judging

Language Focus:
Longer Listening with Notetaking

10 Speaking Style   78
Debate Focus:
Voice, Gestures, Body Language, Facial Expressions

Language Focus:
Word Stress, Emphasis, Imbedded Quotations, Non-verbal Communication

Some Resolutions for Debate   86

Preface

Competitive student debate has long enjoyed great popularity in the English-speaking world. In recent years, we've also seen more and more non-English-speaking countries join the debate community. This internationalization has given debate a new dimension. Now, teachers look to debate to teach language skills, in addition to logic, leadership, and critical thinking. Increasingly, it is the EFL teachers, rather than the social studies teachers, who are setting up debate leagues for their students.

Make Your Point! bridges the gap between debate and EFL. To make this connection, each chapter contains both a **language focus** and a **debate focus**, and develops them in an integrated manner. Debate theory is taught from the very beginning, along with the language skills needed to put the theory into practice.

There are many kinds of debate, including parliamentary, academic, and Lincoln-Douglas. *Make Your Point!* shows a variety of formats, but primarily focuses on **parliamentary debate**. This focus is for three reasons: first, parliamentary is the most popular style internationally; second, parliamentary resembles everyday dialogue more than others; and third, it is the simplest form, with the fewest rules. Indeed, parliamentary debate is very similar to **basic debate**, which many American debate coaches use to train their novices.

Make Your Point! contains the following components:

Student's Book: The student's book has ten chapters, each requiring about six to eight classroom hours, along with an appendix of over eighty sample debate topics. Each chapter includes:

> **Fighting Words**: A vocabulary building section for new words in the chapter. This section features definition, derivation, and listening exercises, including a page of *manga*.
> **Lesson Focus**: A reading section, with comprehension check exercises, that presents a new debate skill.
> **Task Chain**: A series of exercises that build the debate skill from the Lesson Focus, and along with related language skills. Each task chain includes reading, writing, speaking and listening exercises, with a balance of individual, pair and group work.
> **Making It Happen**: A series of exercises to: (a) have students perform the chapter's debate skill, (b) review the vocabulary, and (c) check comprehension and motivate the next section.

CD: The CD contains the spoken material for all the listening tasks in the Student's Book. It may be copied to a tape if necessary.

Teacher's Resources: The *Make your Point* Website, at <http://come.to/makeyourpoint>offers teacher's notes, including a transcript of the CD, an answer key, and feedback from other instructors.

Students should also have access to a **monolingual learner's dictionary**. It's best that a class use a variety of dictionaries, since some may not include the more technical debate vocabulary.

Make Your Point! seeks to make the world of debate accessible, to both students and teachers, in an interesting and exciting way. The author and publishers hope you will enjoy *Make Your Point!*, and will let us know how it has worked for you. Good luck!

1 What is Debate?

FIGHTING WORDS

1. Words in Words

Work with a partner. Match these words with their meanings.
You may use an English-English dictionary for hints. Use these phrases:

What does _____ mean?
I think _____ means _____.
I think so too.
I don't think so. I think _____ means _____.

1. agree
2. opinion
3. express
4. subject
5. decide
6. evaluate
7. form

A. what you are talking about
B. what you believe
C. believe the same thing
D. choose
E. make
F. choose which is good and which is bad
G. say

2. Words about Words

In English, there are many **parts of speech**. Parts of speech means "kinds of words," for example, nouns, verbs, adjectives, adverbs, articles, pronouns, and so forth. The most important are **nouns** and **verbs**.

> A **noun** is a person, place or thing, such as *book, chair, pen* or *table*.
> A **verb** is an action, such as *eat, sleep, walk, run* or *study*.

Look at the new words in exercise **1**. Work with a partner, and decide which are verbs, and which are nouns. Use these sentences:

Is _____ a noun or a verb?
I think _____ is a noun. / I think _____ is a verb.
I think so too. / I don't think so.

3. At a Loss for Words

Fill in the blanks with words from the last page.
Listen to the conversation to check your answers.

lesson focus

Read carefully, and answer the **Questions**.

Everyone has **opinions**. Opinions are what you think or believe. Some people like cats. Some people don't. Some people think students should wear uniforms. Some people think students should choose their own clothes. Some people like tea. Some people like coffee. Some people like both tea and coffee. Some people don't like tea or coffee.

When two people have the same opinion on a subject, they **agree**. When two people have different opinions, they **disagree**. Often, people have different opinions and talk about them. One person expresses his or her opinion, and says why he or she believes it. The other person then expresses another opinion and says why it is better. There are three ways to talk about opinions: they are **argument**, **discussion** and **debate**.

In an **argument**, both people are very angry. They speak very loudly, and they don't listen much to the other person.

In a **discussion**, both people have opinions, but their opinions may change. Each person listens to the other very carefully. They try to agree as much as possible.

In a **debate**, both people have an opinion and their opinions do not change. Each person expresses his or her opinion and says why other opinions are wrong. Usually, there are other people listening to the debate. After the debate, these other people will decide which opinion they agree with more.

Questions:

1. Do you ever have arguments? With whom? Over what subjects?

2. Do you ever have discussions? With whom? Over what subjects?

3. Have you ever seen a debate? Have you ever been in a debate? What was the subject?

Student debate is very popular in many countries. The most famous tournament is the World Universities Debating Championships, held in January every year. At the last Worlds, over 250 teams from 23 countries came. Worlds has been hosted in Canada, the United States, the United Kingdom, Australia, South Africa, Ireland and Greece.

Why do so many students debate? Debate skills are very important, and they help you in everyday life. In debate, you have to express your opinions clearly. If you want to express your ideas clearly, you have to think clearly. In debate, you have to look at a lot of information, evaluate it, and form opinions. In debate, you don't have a lot of time, so you also have to think quickly. These are skills that you use every day.

4. When do you express your opinions? On what subjects?

5. Do you ever have to form opinions quickly? On what subjects?

People who form opinions quickly, and express their opinions clearly, are often very popular. Therefore, debate also teaches you **leadership**. Leadership means that other people think your opinions are good, and they want you to be the boss. If you have good leadership, you will do well in your clubs and job.

6. Do you know people with good leadership skills? Do they express their opinions clearly? Do they think quickly? Why are they good leaders?

Debate is very important in democracy. In non-democratic countries, only one person, or a small group of people, make the country's decisions. But in democratic countries, **popular opinion** is very important. Popular opinion means the opinion of most people about a subject. Popular opinions, however, are not always good opinions. In a democratic country, people can talk about bad popular opinions, and try to change them. A democratic country needs people who can express their opinions strongly and clearly. It is also very important that everyone else listen to their opinions, and choose the best ones.

7. Look at a newspaper. What are some important subjects in your country? Are there different opinions about these subjects? Which opinions do you agree with?

Task Chain

1. Your Opinions

A. What do you think about these subjects? Do you agree or disagree?

	Agree	Disagree
1. Students should wear uniforms.	❑	❑
2. Cats are better pets than dogs.	❑	❑
3. It is OK to eat meat.	❑	❑
4. It is better to live in the city than the country.	❑	❑
5. English is easy.	❑	❑

B. Now write four more opinions. Do you agree or disagree?

_____ ❑ ❑
_____ ❑ ❑
_____ ❑ ❑
_____ ❑ ❑

C. Find another person, and express an opinion. The other person says "I agree." or "I don't agree." Then find another person. Express an opinion to 5 other people.
Use sentences like these:
   I believe students should wear uniforms.
   I don't believe it's OK to eat meat.
   I agree. / I don't agree.

2. What's the Subject?

Listen to four conversations. In each conversation, two people are expressing opinions about a subject. What is the subject of each conversation?

1. Subject: _____

2. Subject: _____

3. Subject: _____

4. Subject: _____

3. More Parts of Speech

Before, we studied nouns and verbs. A noun is a person, place or thing; a verb is an action. Two other important parts of speech are adjectives and adverbs.

An **adjective** is a word that gives information about a noun, such as:
big, fast, blue, rich, beautiful, hot.
An **adverb** is a word that gives information about a verb or adjective, such as:
well, badly, very, quickly, strongly.

In groups of 4, how many nouns can you write down in 30 seconds? How many verbs? How many adjectives? How many adverbs?

4. Reading for Parts of Speech

With a partner, read this paragraph. Make 4 lists, one of the nouns, verbs, adjectives and adverbs. Use these phrases:
What kind of word is _____?
I think _____ is a noun/verb/adjective/adverb.

Sometimes, debates are very short; but not always. In Canada, one of the most famous debates took 3 years. The subject was the Canadian flag. Before 1965, Canada used a flag similar to the British flag. The Prime Minister, Lester Pearson, wanted a totally different flag. But people could not agree on the new flag, so the debate went very slowly. Finally, on February 16, 1965, Canada decided on its new flag, which it still uses now.

5. Listening for Different Parts of Speech

A. A student is giving a short speech. Listen, and list the nouns.
B. Listen again, and list the verbs.
C. Listen once more, and list the adjectives.

6. Deriving Words

A. In English, we often change nouns into verbs, nouns into adjectives, verbs into adjectives, and so on. We do this by changing the last letters of the word. Changing old words into new words is called **deriving** new words.
For example, look at the noun *argument*:
When 2 people fight with words, they _argue_.
A subject about which people have many different opinions is _arguable_.
A person who likes to argue is _argumentative_.

B. From the new words on page 6, derive adjectives. Use an English dictionary. How do you find adjectives in your dictionary? First, look for a noun or verb with a similar meaning. Next to the word, look for "n." or "v." "N." means "noun," and "v." means "verb." Then look at other words near the noun or verb. Look for a word with "adj." written next to it. "Adj." means "adjective." Read the definition. Is it the right word?
  1. A person who strongly believes in many things is _____.
  2. A person who often shows emotion is _____.
  3. Something that will not change is _____.
  4. Something that everyone believes or accepts is _____.

C. Now use your dictionary to derive nouns. Look for "n." in your dictionary.
  1. When everyone believes the same thing, they have an _____.
  2. A common group of words together is an _____.
  3. When you choose something, you make a _____.

7. Definitions

In a debate, you don't have enough time to use your dictionary. If you don't know a word in English, you can make a **definition** of the word.

A. With a partner, match the words with their definition:
  1. kangaroo   A. a place where you borrow money
  2. bank   B. the rules of a country
  3. car   C. a large Australian animal that jumps
  4. law   D. a big machine that you sit inside and drive

B. With a new partner, fill in the missing words in these definitions. You may put more than one word in each blank.
  1. doctor   A. a person who _____
  2. dictionary   B. _____ that lists words and definitions
  3. cocoa   C. the plant that _____ comes from
  4. government   D. the people that debate, make and change _____

8. Listening for Definitions

Listen to the definitions. What are they defining?

  1. _____   2. _____   3. _____   4. _____

MAKING IT HAPPEN

1. Application

A. **Definition game**. Form teams. Each team chooses any 10 words and writes definitions. Each team reads one definition. The first team to guess the word gets a point. The team that wrote the definition also gets a point. If no one understands the definition, no one gets a point.

B. **Derivation game**. Each team makes a list of any 10 words, and gets an English-English dictionary. Each team says one of its words. The first team to find a derived word gets a point. If they can make a sentence with the derived word, they get an extra point.

2. Words and Phrases — Review

A. Look at the 21 words and expressions below. Circle the words you know.

agree	*decision*	*express*
subject	*agreed*	*evaluate*
form	*law*	*verb*
adjective	*adverb*	*argument*
discussion	*noun*	*leadership*
popular opinion	*decide*	*argumentative*
government	*opinion*	*opinionated*

B. Write down 5 more new words that you learned in this chapter. Write a sentence with each word.

3. Questions for Discussion

A. Why are you studying debate?

B. What skills does debating teach? Which of these skills do you have now? Which skills do you want to learn most?

C. In this chapter, we studied Canada's flag debate and America's Lincoln-Douglas debates. What are some famous debates in your country's history?

2 Tennis Debate

FIGHTING WORDS

1. Words in Words

A. With a partner, match these words with their meanings. Use a dictionary.

1. affirm
2. negate
3. topic
4. respond
5. explain
6. reason
7. continue

A. give information to help someone understand
B. agree / say "yes"
C. disagree / say "no"
D. answer / speak about what someone else has said
E. why something is true
F. not stop / start again after stopping
G. subject

B. Work with a partner. Which words are nouns? verbs?

2. Words from Words

A. From the new words, make adjectives. Use a dictionary.
1. In a debate, the team that says "yes" to the topic is the _____ team.
2. In a debate, the team that says "no" to the topic is the _____ team.
3. Something near to a subject is _____.
4. An opinion that has good reasons is a _____ opinion.
5. If you ask for help, a kind person who answers you is _____.

B. From the new words, make nouns. Again, use your dictionary.
1. When you say "yes," you make an _____.
2. Information that helps you understand an opinion is an _____.
3. When you answer someone, you make a _____.
4. Someone who answers is a _____.
5. The opposite of something is its _____.

3. At a Loss for Words

Fill in the blanks with words from the last page.
Listen to the conversation to check your answers.

Lesson focus

Read carefully, and do the **Exercises**.

There are many different kinds of debate. In some debates, you debate against only one person. Other times, you are on a team and against another team. Teams sometimes have 2 people, sometimes 3 or 4. Sometimes, the same team speaks first and last; other times, one team speaks first and the other team speaks last. In some debates, speeches last 5 minutes; in other debates, they last up to 12. In this chapter, we will learn a very simple kind of debate called "**tennis debating**."

In a tennis debate, there are two teams, called the **affirmative** team and the **negative** team. Each team has between 2 and 6 people. There is a simple topic, such as "Dogs are better than cats," or "The city is better than the country." The affirmative team agrees with the topic, and the negative team disagrees.

Each team talks about the topic, and writes down 10 reasons for their opinion.

When the teams are finished, they sit across from each other. The affirmative team begins. One person from the affirmative team (anyone is OK) reads one reason from their list, and explains it. Someone from the negative (anyone is OK) then responds. The negative person may say that the affirmative reason is not true or not important. Anyone from the affirmative team then can respond to the negative. Anyone from the negative team can respond again. Nobody has to speak; anyone who wants to speak may speak. The debate continues until nobody wants to speak about that reason.

Then it is the negative's turn. Someone from the negative team (anyone is OK) reads one reason from their list, and explains it. Someone from the affirmative (anyone is OK) then responds. They may say that the negative reason is not true or not important. Someone from the negative team then can respond to the affirmative. Someone from the affirmative team can respond again. Again, nobody has to speak; anyone who wants to speak may. The debate continues until nobody wants to speak about that reason.

Repeat again with the affirmative, then the negative, then the affirmative, then the negative, until the debate time is over.

How many reasons can you write down? For example, suppose the topic is "The city is better than the country." The affirmative team can say:
    Cities have many interesting restaurants; the country doesn't.
    The city is more exciting than the country.

Exercise 1

A. Write 2 more reasons why the city is better.

B. Now, write 3 reasons why the country is better.

How can you explain your reasons? Sometimes, you can give examples. For example, suppose the topic is "Cats are better than dogs." One affirmative reason is that "Cats catch mice, but dogs don't." Someone can explain, "I have a cat, and my cat often catches mice. Have you ever heard of a dog catching mice?"

Sometimes, you explain a reason with **conditional sentences**. A conditional sentence is a sentence with the word "if." For example, suppose the topic is "Baseball is better than soccer." One negative reason is, "Baseball is more dangerous than soccer." Someone can explain, "If a soccer ball hits your head, you'll be OK. But if a baseball hits your head, you can be hurt very badly."

Exercise 2
Write explanations for your reasons from Exercise 1.

How can you respond to the other team's reasons? Suppose the topic is "Dogs are better than cats," and you are on the negative team. You can do 3 things. First, you can say that the reason is not true. For example, if the other team says "Dogs are quieter than cats," you can respond, "No, they aren't. Dogs are much noisier than cats. For example......"

Second, you can say that the reason is not important. For example, if the other team says, "Dogs have bigger feet than cats," you can respond, "So what? Big feet and small feet are both OK." Third, you can say that the reason is true, but you have a better reason. For example, if the other team says, "Dogs protect your home from thieves, but cats don't," you can respond, "Yes, but cats catch mice, and dogs don't. In our country, mice are a bigger problem then thieves."

Exercise 3
Write responses to your reasons from Exercise 1.

Task Chain

1. Comparisons with Adjectives

A. Compare dogs and cats. Write sentences like the examples.
- fun — *Dogs are more fun than cats.*
- large — *Dogs are larger than cats.*
1. noisy _____
2. smart _____
3. interesting _____
4. friendly _____

B. With a partner, write 4 more sentences like this about dogs and cats.

2. Comparisons with Adverbs

A. Again, compare dogs and cats. Make sentences like the examples.
- long — Dogs live *longer* than cats.
- often — Dogs play *more often* than cats.
1. high — Cats jump _____ than dogs.
2. fast — Dogs run _____ than cats.
3. good — Dogs protect _____ than cats.
4. far — Cats can fall _____ than dogs.

B. With a partner, write 4 more sentences like this about dogs and cats.

3. Listening for Comparisons

Listen. Charlie and Julie are comparing soccer and baseball. What do they say?
1. There is more _____ in soccer than in baseball.
2. Soccer teams are _____ than baseball teams.
3. Soccer players can run _____.
4. Baseball games stop _____.
5. Soccer scores _____.
6. Soccer rules _____.
7. More people _____.
8. In America, _____.
9. _____.
10. _____.

4. Contrasts

A. Contrast summer and winter. Fill in the missing words:
- Summer is hot; *winter isn't*.
- In the winter, we can go skiing; *in the summer, we can't*.
1. In the winter, we go to school; _____.
2. In the winter, there is a lot of snow; _____.
3. In the summer, beaches are open; _____.
4. In the winter, we must wear warm clothes; _____.

B. With a partner, write 4 more sentences like this about summer and winter.

5. More Fighting Words

A. Look at these words: *definite*, *probable*, and *possible*.
Definite means 100% will happen, for example: "The sun will rise tomorrow."
Probable means 80-99% will happen, for example: "My TV will work tonight."
Possible means can happen, 1-100% for example: "The sun will rise tomorrow." or "I will have 7 children."

B. Match these 3 more words with their meanings:
1. indefinite   A. cannot happen
2. improbable   B. maybe will happen, maybe will not happen
3. impossible   C. can happen, but it would be a surprise.

6. Definite, Probable, or Improbable

A. With a partner, decide if these sentences are definite, probable or improbable. Use these sentences:
   *I think that "High schools will stop having tests." is **improbable**.*
   *I think that "Smoking is bad for your health." is **definite**.*
   *I think so too. / I don't think so. I think it's **probable**.*

- High schools will stop having tests. → *improbable*
- Smoking is bad for your health. → *definite*

1. It will rain tomorrow. → _____
2. It will snow tomorrow. → _____
3. The trains will be late tonight. → _____
4. Someone in the class will get married. → _____
5. Brazil will win the next World Cup in soccer. → _____
6. Someone in the class will have 15 children. → _____
7. Winter will come next year. → _____
8. There will be a big earthquake in Japan in the future. → _____

B. With your partner, write down 3 more things that are definite, 3 more things that are probable, and 3 more things that are improbable.

C. Change partners, and show your list to your new partner. Does your partner agree?

7. Conditional Sentences

"Conditional" means "indefinite." A "conditional sentence" is a sentence with the word "if." Look at these two examples:

>(probable) *If it **rains** tomorrow, **I'll** take an umbrella.*
>(improbable) *If it **rained** tomorrow, **I'd** take an umbrella.*

Whether something is probable or improbable is very important in English.
Using the examples, fill in the missing words.
1. If a baseball ___ (hit) your head, you _____ (have) a headache.
2. If schools _____ (don't have) tests, students _____ (be) very happy.
3. If there _____ (be) a big earthquake in Tokyo, many people _____ (die).
4. If I _____ (win) a lot of money, I _____ (buy) many presents.
5. If I _____ (go) to the store tonight, I _____ (buy) some sweets.
6. If I _____ (have) time on Sunday, I _____ (go) shopping.

8. Conditional Questions

A. A conditional question is a question with the word "if." Ask a partner these questions:

1. If it rains on Saturday, what will you do?
2. If you won a lot of money, what would you buy?
3. If you meet your friends this weekend, where will you go?
4. If you had a part-time job, what would you spend less time doing?

B. Now ask 4 more conditional questions.

9. Listening for Conditionals

A. Ray and Katie are in a tennis debate on the topic: "High school students should not have part-time jobs." Listen once. Who is on the affirmative team? Who is on the negative team?

B. Listen again. How many conditional sentences do you hear?
Ray: ____ Katie: ____

C. Write down the conditionals in the debate. Who says each one?
1. If they have part-time jobs, they _____.
2. If they spend less time studying, _____.
3. If _____, _____.
4. If _____, _____.
5. If _____, _____.

Making It Happen

1. Application

Choose two of these topics, and hold tennis debates on them.
Cats are better pets than dogs.
It is better to live in the country than the city.
Students should not have uniforms.
There should be no school on Saturday.
Mountain vacations are better than sea vacations.
It is better to be an only child than to have brothers and sisters.

2. Words and Phrases — Review

A. Look at the 21 words below. Circle the words that you know.

affirm	*negation*	*improbable*
negate	*explanation*	*topical*
topic	*response*	*reasonable*
respond	*possible*	*reason*
impossible	*continue*	*definite*
affirmative	*indefinite*	*affirmation*
probable	*negative*	*explain*

B. Write a story with no more than 100 words. Use as many of these words as you can. How many of these words can you use?

C. Write down 5 more new words that you learned in this chapter. Use each word in a sentence.

3. Questions for Discussion

A. In English, conditional sentences for probable things are different than for improbable things. Is your language the same way?

B. There are many debate styles. What are the good points of the tennis debate style? What are the bad points?

C. What other topics would you like to debate about?

3 Resolutions and Cases

FIGHTING WORDS

1. Words in Words

A. With a partner, match these words with their meanings. Use a dictionary.

1. abolish
2. propose
3. oppose
4. vague
5. public
6. protect
7. endangered

A. disagree / fight
B. managed by the government
C. could all die
D. stop something / end something
E. guard
F. suggest strongly
G. not clear / has many different meanings

B. Work with a partner. Which words are verbs? adjectives?

2. Words from Words

A. From the new words, make nouns. Use a dictionary.

1. A person who wants to end something is an _____.
2. When you want to end something, you want its _____.
3. If you want to do something, and tell other people, you make a _____.
4. A person who strongly agrees with something is a _____.
5. A person who disagrees with something is an _____.
6. If you think we should only buy things made in this country, you are a _____.

B. Some animals are very rare, and may all die. These animals are called **endangered species**. What are some endangered species? Why are they endangered?

3. At a Loss for Words

Fill in the blanks with words from the last page. Listen to the conversation to check your answers.

lesson focus

Read carefully, and do the **Exercise**.

Every debate starts with the **resolution**. Some examples of resolutions are:

Resolved: Restaurants should not use wood chopsticks.
Resolved: School uniforms should be abolished.
Resolved: Asia is a better place to live than America.

The affirmative team says that the resolution is true. The negative team says that the resolution is false. In other words, the affirmative team **proposes** the resolution, and the negative team **opposes** the resolution.

Sometimes, the resolution is very clear. But other times, resolutions have **vague** parts. For example, look at the resolution, "Resolved: School uniforms should be abolished." What does "school uniforms" mean? Does it mean all school uniforms, or only high-school uniforms, or maybe only public school uniforms? How about "be abolished"? Who should abolish school uniforms? Should the government make a law, or should each school decide by itself?

If a resolution has vague parts, then the two teams may understand the resolution differently. For example, one team may talk about public high schools, while the other team may talk about private universities. This makes a poor debate, since the teams are not talking about the same topic.

Therefore, the affirmative team has the **burden of definition**. In other words, it must find the important vague points, and make them clear. This is called **making a case**.

For example, look at the resolution: "Resolved: We should help animals more."
Here are some vague points:

1. *Who is "we"?*
   The national government? The city government? Community groups? Every person?
2. *Which "animals"?*
   Pets? Animals that people eat? Animals used in science? Endangered species?
3. *What does "help" mean?*
   Make laws? Protect land? Take home a stray pet?

The affirmative team can choose the case they want to propose. For example, they may choose any of these cases:

1. The city government should build more animal shelters.
2. Our country should abolish all imports of ivory.
3. Making jobs is more important than protecting endangered species.
4. Every family should take in a stray pet.

The affirmative must choose only one case, and must explain its case at the beginning of the debate. The case then becomes the topic of the debate.

Although the affirmative team may choose the case, there are three rules:

Rule 1: The case must be clear. The case must not have any important vague points.

Rule 2: The case must be **arguable**. In other words, the negative team must have good reasons.

Rule 3: The case must be from the resolution. The affirmative team cannot talk about a completely different subject.

Exercise

Here are some bad cases from the resolution: *Resolved: We should help animals more.* Why is each case bad?

1. The national government should do something to help stray animals.
2. Beating little dogs is not nice.
3. Hamburgers are better than hot dogs.
4. Pandas should be protected.
5. Some animals are very cute.

If the affirmative team makes a good case, then the case becomes the topic of the debate. The affirmative team must not change its case, or make a new case, during the debate. The negative team must oppose the affirmative's case, and not a different case from the resolution.

Task Chain

1. More Fighting Words

A. With a partner, match these words to their meanings. Use a dictionary.

1. clarify
2. diagram
3. capital
4. free
5. examination
6. environment
7. option

A. choice
B. picture
C. can choose
D. big test
E. where the government is
F. make clear
G. air, land, water, and living things

B. From the new words, derive more new words. Use a dictionary.

1. An explanation about a vague subject is a _____.
2. If you can say anything you want, you have _____ of speech.
3. If you have to do something, it's compulsory, but if you can choose to do it or not do it, it is _____.
4. A person who wants to protect nature is an _____.
5. When you study something very carefully, you _____ it.

2. Good Cases — Bad Cases

Good cases are clear and arguable. With a partner, decide if these cases are good. Under the words *Clear*, *Arguable* and *Good Case*, write ✓ for "yes" and ✗ for "no." Use these sentences:

Is this case clear or vague?
  I think it is clear.
  I think it's vague, because _____ can mean many things.
Is this case arguable?
  I think it is arguable. Both teams have good reasons.
  I think it is not arguable. The negative team has no good reasons.

	Clear	+	Arguable	=	Good Case
High school students should wear uniforms.	✓	+	✓	=	✓
Smoking is bad for your health.	✓	+	✗	=	✗
1. Our country should not move its capital.		+		=	
2. Children should never drink whiskey.		+		=	
3. We should help our neighbors.		+		=	
4. Students should usually do their homework.		+		=	
5. People should never eat meat.		+		=	

3. Brainstorming

A. Look at the diagram below. It is called a **brainstorming diagram**.

Resolved: We should help animals more.

- *Who is "we"?*
  - individuals
  - the national government
  - our school
  - ___
  - ___

- *How?*
  - stop eating meat
  - build shelters
  - take strays in our homes
  - ___
  - ___

- *Which animals?*
  - dogs and cats
  - pandas
  - elephants
  - ___
  - ___

Possible Cases:
Everyone should become a vegetarian.
The city should make more animal shelters.
___
___

B. Listen, and practice this conversation:

Mike: The resolution is "We should help animals more." What are the vague points?
Julie: I think "we" is vague. What can it mean?
Mike: It can mean "people" or "the government."
Julie: "Government" is also vague. What kind of government?
Mike: The national government or the city government.
Julie: The city government...hmmm.....I know! One possible case is: "The city government should build more animal shelters."
Mike: Good idea! I'll write it down.

C. In pairs, finish the diagram in part **A**.

4. Listening for Brainstorming

John and Mary are brainstorming the resolution:
  Resolved: Students need more freedom.
Listen to their conversation, and draw their brainstorming diagram.

5. Brainstorming Resolutions

Now, look at these resolutions. In groups, make brainstorming diagrams for each resolution. Make at least 3 cases for each resolution.

1. Resolved: The environment must be protected.
2. Resolved: Rich countries should help poor countries more.
3. Resolved: Entrance examinations should be abolished.

6. Paraphrasing

Paraphrase means "say in a different way." Read these cases:

1. People should become vegetarians.
2. The government should abolish the import of ivory.
3. The city should make more animal shelters.
4. High school students should not have to study math.

When you make a case, you should always try to paraphrase it. This helps everybody understand the case. With a partner, match the cases above with their paraphrases below.

A. Customs officers should stop anyone bringing ivory into this country.
B. The local government should make more centers for stray dogs and cats.
C. Math should be optional in high school.
D. Everyone should stop eating meat.

7. Listening for Paraphrases

Look at the cases below. Each of them has been paraphrased. First, listen to the paraphrase, and match it to the case. Then listen again, and write the paraphrase under the case. The first (A.) has been done for you.

A. High school students should be allowed to have part-time jobs.
_____

B. Restaurants should not use wooden chopsticks.
_____

C. English should be compulsory from primary school.
_____

D. In public schools, summer vacations should last 3 months.
There should be no classes at government-run schools from June to September.

E. Cats are better pets than dogs.
_____

MAKING IT HAPPEN

1. Application

For each of the following resolutions, brainstorm and make 3 cases. Then paraphrase each case.
1. *Resolved:* People should do more sports.
2. *Resolved:* Students should study other countries more closely.
3. *Resolved:* The government should improve public transportation.

2. Words and Phrases — Review

A. Look at the 21 words below. Circle the words that you know.

abolish	*propose*	*opponent*
vague	*public*	*abolitionist*
endangered	*proposal*	*protect*
oppose	*clarify*	*optional*
diagram	*freedom*	*environment*
option	*capital*	*free*
examine	*environmentalist*	*proponent*

B. Put these words into groups. Each group should have between 4 and 7 words. Make any groups that will help you remember the words.

C. Write down 5 more new words that you learned in this chapter. Write down what each word means.

3. Questions for Discussion

A. Usually, the affirmative team can choose the case. Is this fair? What is the biggest problem with this rule? How can we fix this problem?

B. In some debate rules, if the negative team does not like the affirmative case, they may give a completely different case. The two teams then argue about which case is "closer to the resolution." Is this a good debate? Why or why not?

4 Points

FIGHTING WORDS

1. Words in Words

A. With a partner, match these words with their meanings. Use a dictionary.

1. prove
2. judge
3. quote
4. intelligent
5. connect
6. emotional
7. save

A. decide which is right and which is wrong
B. show why two things are related
C. keep for later / protect
D. repeat something that another person said
E. very smart
F. show definitely that something is true
G. with strong feelings

B. Work with a partner. Which words are verbs? adjectives?

2. Words from Words

A. From the new words, derive nouns. Use a dictionary.
1. Happiness, sadness, anger, are examples of _____.
2. The person who decides who wins a debate is the _____.
3. Another word for "decision" is _____.
4. Something a famous person said is a _____.
5. The ability to understand many things is _____.
6. If you need help, and another person helps you, that person is your _____.
7. If two things are related, they have a _____.

B. From the new words, derive adjectives. Again use your dictionary.
1. A person who usually makes good decisions is _____.
2. A person who often finds bad things in other people is _____.
3. A country's system of laws and courts is the _____ system.
4. If you show that "x" is true, and everyone agrees, "x" is _____.
5. Something that can be understood is _____.

3. At a Loss for Words

Fill in the blanks with words from the last page. Listen to the conversation to check your answers.

Lesson Focus

Read carefully, and do the **Exercises**.

In a debate, you have to give reasons to prove your case. For example, if you are on the affirmative team, and your case is, "Cats are better pets than dogs." Your reasons may be:

- A. Cats are smarter than dogs.
- B. Cats are quieter than dogs.
- C. Cats are cheaper to keep than dogs.

Each of these reasons is called a **point**. Points are very important in debate, and you must make your points clearly. When you make a point, you should follow four steps:

- **Step 1:** Give your point a **signpost.**
- **Step 2:** Explain the point.
- **Step 3:** Connect the point to the case.
- **Step 4:** **Impact** your point.

Step 1: A **signpost** is a name for your point, such as *intelligence*, *beauty*, *freedom*, *peace*, *cost*, *democracy*, or *education*. It should have no more than 3 words. If you give your point an easy name, it is easy to write down and understand. Your signpost should be a noun. If you don't know a good noun, but you know a good adjective or verb, use your dictionary to derive a good noun.

Step 2: After you give your signpost, you must explain the point. You have to say why the point is true, and perhaps give some examples.

Step 3: Then, you must connect the point to your case. Remember, you win a debate by proving your case, not by making a lot of points.

Step 4: Finally, you should **impact** your point. An impact is something that helps the judge remember the point. For example, it can be a famous quotation, a funny story or joke, a popular expression, or an emotional example.

So let's look at our case that "Cats are better pets than dogs." Our first point was, "Cats are smarter than dogs." Let's give this point the signpost, "intelligence." Here is a well-made point:

> *(step 1) Our first point is "intelligence." (step 2) Cats are much smarter than dogs. If they get lost, they can find their way home. If you go on vacation, you can leave food and they'll save it. Dogs are not smart. They often get lost. They eat everything very quickly. (step 3) Smart pets are easier to keep and more interesting; therefore, cats are better pets than dogs. (step 4) I once saw a dog run in circles for 10 minutes, because it wanted to catch its own tail. How foolish!*

Exercise 1   Our second point was "Cats are quieter than dogs."
Read the point, and think of a good signpost.

> *(step 1) Our second point is _____. (step 2) Cats are much quieter than dogs. Dogs are very noisy. They bark all the time, and they make your neighbors angry. Cats, however, are usually very quiet. When you play with them, they purr softly. It's a good feeling. When you play with dogs, they often bark, and may bite you. (step 3) We believe that quiet pets are better pets, because they make your life more peaceful. Since cats are quieter than dogs, they make better pets. (step 4) Do you like being woken up at 3 o'clock in the morning by a noisy dog?*

Exercise 2   Our third point was "Cats are cheaper to keep than dogs."
Read the point, and think of a good signpost.

> *(step 1) Our third point is _____. (step 2) Cats are cheaper to keep than dogs. If you go on vacation for a short time, you must pay someone to look after your dog. Cats can be left alone. Also, cats don't eat much, but dogs eat hundreds of dollars a month in food. (step 3) Cheaper pets are better, because you can save money. Since cats are cheaper to keep than dogs, we think that cats are better pets. (step 4) A big dog can cost 200 dollars a month to feed. That's over 1000 dollars a year! For that money, you can fly to Europe!*

Task Chain

1. More Fighting Words

A. With a partner, match these words with their meaning.

1. pay attention
2. improve
3. comfortable
4. useless
5. spend
6. coordinated
7. classical

A. with no pain or bad feeling
B. doesn't help you at all
C. can work together well
D. from old times
E. listen carefully
F. become better
G. pay / use

B. Use these words in this conversation:

Ray: What's your favorite subject?
Jane: I love art. I think it's really interesting!
Ray: Really? I don't. It's a ¹._____ subject, and the teacher is boring. It's hard for me to ²._____ in class. I always want to go to sleep!
Jane: Art is not ³._____ — it is important to understand our culture. And I love painting!
Ray: I'm bad at painting. My fingers are not ⁴._____ at all. One time, I got paint all over my uniform. I had to ⁵._____ a lot of money to buy a new one.
Jane: Painting can be difficult, but if you practice, you will ⁶._____.
Ray: Ha! I don't even like the classroom. My chair isn't ⁷._____ at all.

2. Making Signposts

Read this point. Think of a good signpost, then mark the point with (step 1), (step 2), (step 3) and (step 4).

Case: Classical languages should not be studied in high schools.

> Our first point is _____. Classical languages take a very long time to learn. Students have to learn many new words, and spend lots of time reading stories. Students should use the time to study English, math or science, so that they can get better jobs, and make our country stronger. If we stop studying classical languages, we make ourselves and our country richer. We need engineers, scientists and translators much more than classicists. Americans have stopped studying Latin and Greek; we should do the same.

3. What's Missing?

A. Read these points. Try to mark the points with **(step 1)**, **(step 2)**, **(step 3)** and **(step 4)**. In each point, one of the steps is missing. Which one?

1. Case: Chopsticks are better than forks.

Our first point is, "coordination." Forks are very simple — even a monkey can use them. To use chopsticks, your fingers must be coordinated. Coordination is very important — since we use our hands every day. Uncoordinated people are very dangerous — when they cut a cake, they may cut off their hand!

2. Case: High school students should not wear uniforms.

Our first point is "comfort." If there were no uniforms, students would be more comfortable and enjoy school more. They would pay more attention in class, and learn much more. Can you pay attention when you are sweating or shivering?

3. Case: Japan should move its capital.

Our first point is, "earthquakes." Tokyo has big earthquakes about every 70 years. Since the last big earthquake was in 1923, the next one could be very soon. In a large earthquake, the government has to work very quickly. It has to repair the train, telephone, electricity and water lines. It has to send food and medicine. It has to help people who are under buildings. But if the government is in Tokyo during the earthquake, government workers will not be able to work. They will not be able to talk to each other and make decisions. If the government is in another place, they will be able to help.

B. Re-write the points with the missing steps put in.

4. Listening for Signposts

A debater is proving the case that, "You should take your next vacation in America." He has 3 points. What are his signposts?

Signpost 1: _____   Signpost 2: _____   Signpost 3: _____

5. Flowing

A. Look at this point again, and circle the important words in each sentence.

Case: Cats are better than dogs.

> Our (first) point is ("intelligence.") Cats are much smarter than dogs. If they get lost, they can find their way home. If you go on vacation, you can leave food and they'll save it. Dogs are not smart. They often get lost, and they eat everything very quickly. Smart pets are easier to keep and more interesting; therefore, cats are better than dogs. I once saw a dog run in circles for 10 minutes, because it wanted to catch its own tail. How foolish!

B. Now look at this diagram. It is a **flow** of the point. In a flow, you write down the signpost, and the important words.

1st: Intelligence →
  cats smarter dogs
  lost → find home
  vacation → leave food, cats save
  dogs: often lost, eat quickly
  smart → easier / interesting → better pets
  dog → circles 10 min → catch tail

C. With a partner, make flows of all the other points in this chapter.

 6. Listening and Flowing

Now listen again to the case that, "You should take your next vacation in America," (page 35). Flow the 3 points.

Hint: When people speak English, they **stress** the important words. Stress means "say more loudly." When you flow a speech, listen for the stressed words.

MAKING IT HAPPEN

1. Application

A. With a partner, write a point affirming each of these cases:
   1. *High school students should wear uniforms.*
   2. *The city should make more animal shelters.*

B. Again with a partner, prepare points affirming these cases. This time, do not write every word. Write only the important words. The cases are:
   1. *You should take your next vacation in Australia.*
   2. *Classical languages should be studied in high school.*
   3. *Everyone should become a vegetarian.*

C. Make your points to other students. Listen to other students' points, and flow them.

D. Use your flows to repeat other students' points.

2. Vocabulary Review

A. Look at the words below. Circle the words that you know.

prove	*save*	*judge*
intelligent	*connect*	*emotional*
quotation	*judicious*	*coordinated*
judicial	*proven*	*judgmental*
intelligence	*comfort*	*connection*
judgment	*spend*	*useless*
pay attention	*improve*	*classical*

B. Write down 7 more new words that you learned in this chapter. Write a conversation with your 7 words.

3. Questions for Discussion

A. Why are signposts important?

B. Imagine that you are on an affirmative team, and you have 3 points. One point is very important, one point is somewhat important, and one point is not-so-important. Which point should you say first? second? third? Why?

5 The 1AC

FIGHTING WORDS

1. Words in Words

A. With a partner, match these words with their meanings. Use a dictionary.

1. construct   A. not more and not less
2. abbreviate   B. build
3. entire   C. affirm / help / agree with
4. state   D. a group of people who listen to something
5. audience   E. make shorter
6. support   F. say
7. exactly   G. complete

B. Which words are nouns? verbs? adjectives? adverbs?

2. Words from Words

A. From the new words, derive adjectives. Use a dictionary.
1. In a debate, a speech that builds a case is called a _____ speech.
2. Something you can hear is _____.
3. Stereos, tape players, and CD players are kinds of _____ equipment.
4. Something that is shorter than usual is _____.
5. A friend that helps you is a _____ friend.
6. A quotation with no changes is an _____ quotation.

B. From the new words, derive nouns. Again, use your dictionary.
1. A group of letters that means a longer word is an _____.
2. A person who helps or agrees with you is a _____.
3. A person that builds houses is a _____ worker.
4. Another expression for "all of it" is "in its _____."
5. A prepared speech is called a _____.
6. A place where people give speeches is an _____.

3. At a Loss for Words

Fill in the blanks with words from the last page.
Listen to the conversation to check your answers.

Lesson Focus

Read carefully, and answer the **Questions** at the end.

In a debate, the first speech is called the **first affirmative constructive speech**. We can abbreviate first affirmative constructive as **1AC**. The 1AC is very important, but it is much easier than the other speeches, since you can prepare it.

When you make a speech, you always speak to the judge. The judge is called "**Mr. Speaker**" or "**Madam Speaker.**" We use "Mr." for a man, and "Madam" for a woman.

The 1AC usually has 3 parts:
1. Link
2. Three or Four Points
3. Conclusion

The **link** takes about 1-2 minutes. The conclusion takes about 30-60 seconds. The rest of the time is for the points.

In the link, you have to clarify the resolution, and state your case. During the link, you have to:

Step 1: Thank the judge and audience
Step 2: Clarify the vague points
Step 3: State your case
Step 4: Paraphrase your case

For example, look at this link:

Resolved: We should help animals more.

> *(step 1) Thank you Mr. Speaker, ladies and gentlemen. (step 2) The resolution is "We should help animals more." The vague points are "we," "help" and "animals." By "we," we mean "all people." By "animals," we mean "all animals." By "help," we mean, "be kind to." Therefore, we believe that "All people should be kind to all animals." However, many people eat animals. This is not kind. (step 3) Therefore, our case is: "All people should stop eating animals." (step 4) In other words, "We should all be vegetarians."*

If the resolution has no vague points, then you don't do **step 2**. For example:

Resolved: Students in our school should not wear uniforms.

> (**step 1**) Thank you Madam Speaker, ladies and gentlemen. (**step 3**) The resolution today is: "Students in our school should not wear uniforms." (**step 4**) In other words, "All students here should be able to choose their own clothes." We strongly affirm this case.

After your link, you give your points. You should have 3 or 4 points. Remember that each point has 4 steps: (a) the signpost, (b) explanation, (c) connection to the case and (d) impact. Usually, your best point should be first, and your second-best point should be last. In a speech, the most important times are the beginning and the end.

At the end of your speech, you make a conclusion. In your conclusion, you should (a) repeat your 3 or 4 signposts, (b) give one more impact and (c) ask the judge and the audience to support you.

Here is an example of a conclusion:

> *Mr. Speaker, in this debate, we have talked about "intelligence," "noise" and "cost." These points show that cats are much better pets than dogs. Please imagine a soft, gentle cat lying in your arms, purring gently. You must agree that cats are the best. For these reasons, we ask you to support our side today.*

If you are on the negative team, you must flow the 1AC very carefully. When the 1AC states the case, you should write the case exactly as it is said. In other words, you should write down every word in the case. For the rest of the speech, you write down only the important words. When you flow, you should use abbreviations for common words and long words. For example, instead of "The United States," you should write "US." Instead of "government," you should write "gvt." If you use abbreviations, you will be able to write more quickly.

Questions:
1. What does link mean?

2. What are you linking?

Task Chain

1. More Fighting Words

A. With a partner, match the words to their meaning. Use a dictionary.

1. dress up
2. locality
3. ban
4. cruelty
5. experience
6. boycott
7. adult

A. a person who is not a child any more
B. learn by seeing or doing something
C. choose not to buy
D. wear nicer clothes than usual
E. area
F. causing pain to a person or animal
G. stop / not allow

B. From the new words, derive more words. Use a dictionary.

1. The city government is also called the _____ government.
2. A person who causes pain to other people or animals is a _____ person.
3. A person who has done a lot of debate is an _____ debater.
4. Your childhood years are your childhood; your adult years are your _____.
5. Another word for "find" is _____.

2. Abbreviations

A. With a partner, read this paragraph. Most of the letters *a*, *e*, *i* and *o* have been taken out. Re-write this paragraph with the letters put back in.

Jewish-Christian Debates in Europe

n th 1300's, n urp, thr wr mny dbts btwn Jws nd Chrstns. Th mst fmus Jwsh-Chrstn dbt ws hld n 1263, n th Spnsh cty f Barcelona. Thr wr nly 2 dbtrs. n th Jwsh sd ws Nachmanides, a fmus tchr. n th Chrstn sd ws Pablo Christiani, wh ws brn a Jw but bcm Chrstn. Mny ppl wtchd th dbt, ncludng th kng nd qun. ftr th dbt, bth th Jws nd Chrstns wrt but th dbt, but thy wrt vry dffrnt thngs. Tdy, nbdy knws wh rlly wn th dbt.

B. Newspapers often use abbreviations, especially in **headlines**. Headlines are the titles in a newspaper. In groups of 3, look through an English newspaper. Write down all the abbreviations you can find. What do they mean?

3. Making Links

Read each of these links, and fill in the missing words, then mark the link with (**step 1**), (**step 2**), (**step 3**) and (**step 4**) as on page 40. Some blank spaces have more than one word. The resolution is: *Resolved: We should help animals more.*

A.

> Thank you Mr. Speaker, ladies and gentlemen. The _____ is "We should help animals more." The vague points are "we," "help" and "animals." By "we," we mean "the people in our _____." By "animals," we mean "stray pets." By "help," we mean "give a place to stay." Therefore, we believe that "Our city should give a place to stay to _____." Therefore, our case is: "Our city should make more _____." In other words, "the local government should make more centers for _____."

B.

> Thank you Mr. Speaker, ladies and gentlemen. Today's _____ is "We should help animals more." The _____ points are "we," "help" and "animals." By "we," _____ "our country's government." By "animals," _____ "elephants." _____ "help," _____ "protect from being killed." Therefore, we believe that "Our country's government should protect elephants from being killed." Many people kill elephants, because they want _____. If we don't use _____, people will not _____. Therefore, our case is: "Our country should ban all imports of _____." In other words, "Customs agents should stop people from bringing _____ into this country."

C.

> Thank you Mr. Speaker, ladies and gentlemen. _____ "We should help animals more." _____ "we," "help" and "animals." _____ "all people." _____ "rabbits." _____ "protect from cruelty." Therefore, we believe that "_____" Now, many companies test their new cosmetics by putting them in rabbits' eyes. If the rabbit goes blind or feels a lot of pain, then they don't sell it. This is very cruel to rabbits. _____ "Everyone should boycott cosmetics that have been tested on rabbits." _____, "We should only buy make-up that has _____ been tested on rabbits."

4. Flowing Links

A. When you flow a link, you should write the important words. Use abbreviations for long or common words. You should try to write the case statement word-for-word. For example, look at the link on page 40. Here is the flow:

Resolved: We should help animals more.
Vg Pts:
    we → all pple
    anmls → all anmls
    hlp → be kind
pple eat anmls → not kind
Case: All pple should stop eating anmls.
    → vegetarians

B. Now look at the 3 links on the previous page. Take flows for these links.

5. Listening for Links

Listen to 3 links from 3 different resolutions. Take flows.

A. *Resolved*: Students should have more freedom.

B. *Resolved*: Rich countries should help poor countries.

C. *Resolved*: People should experience other cultures.

6. Flowing a 1AC

Listen to a 1AC on the resolution, *Resolved: Students should have more freedom.* Flow the speech.

MAKING IT HAPPEN

1. Application

A. In groups of 3, choose any case that you made in Chapter 3. Write and make a 1AC speech in support of the case. Listen to 2 other students' speeches, and flow them.

B. Now choose any other case, and prepare and make a 1AC speech. Do not write the entire speech — just make short notes. Listen to 2 other students' speeches, and flow them.

C. Use your flows to repeat other students' 1AC's.

2. Vocabulary Review

A. Look at the words below. Circle the words that you know.

construct	*exactly*	*support*
abbreviate	*entire*	*audience*
constructive	*locate*	*local*
audio	*supportive*	*abbreviation*
dress up	*adult*	*boycott*
state	*ban*	*cruel*
abbreviated	*experienced*	*audible*

B. Put these words into groups of 3 or 4. Make any group that will help you remember the words.

C. Write down 7 more new words that you learned in this chapter. Write a definition for each word.

3. Questions for Discussion

A. If the 1AC is poor, then often the entire debate is poor. Why?

B. What is the most difficult part of the 1AC speech? How can you make it easier?

6 The 1NC

FIGHTING WORDS

1. Words in Words

A. With a partner, match these words with their meanings. Use your dictionary.

1. strategy   A. fix / repair
2. refute   B. connected to a topic
3. difference   C. say the opposite
4. solve   D. important
5. relevant   E. why 2 things are not the same
6. significant   F. explain why something is not right
7. contradict   G. how you fight

B. Which words are nouns? verbs? adjectives?

2. Words from Words

A. From the new words, derive nouns. Use a dictionary.
   1. Another word for "importance" is _____.
   2. When you say why something is not true, you make a _____.
   3. A person who decides how to fight a battle is a _____.
   4. If you know how to fix a problem, you have a _____.
   5. If something is closely connected to a topic, it has _____.
   6. If two points say opposite things, there is a _____ between them.

B. From the new words, derive adjectives. Again, use your dictionary.
   1. A decision about how to fight something is a _____ decision.
   2. If two things are not the same, they are _____.
   3. Information that disagrees with your opinion is _____ information.
   4. If you can prove that "x" is wrong, then "x" is _____.
   5. If you can fix "x," then "x" is _____.

3. At a Loss for Words

Fill in the blanks with words from the last page.
Listen to the conversation to check your answers.

Lesson Focus

Read carefully, and answer the **Questions**.

The second speech of a debate is called the **first negative constructive** speech. We can abbreviate first negative constructive as **1NC**. Sometimes, there is a 2-5 minute break between the 1AC and the 1NC. This time is called **preparatory time**, or **prep time**. We call it prep time because the negative team uses it to prepare.

During the 1AC and prep time, the negative team has to choose a **negative strategy**. Negative strategy means "how the negative will argue against the case." There are 3 negative strategies: **straight-out opposition**, **technical challenge**, and **countercasing**. Usually, the negative should choose only one strategy.

In straight-out opposition, the negative says that the case is wrong. For example, if the case is, "Our school should change its uniform to a green suit and tie," then the negative team says "No, our school should not change its uniform. The current uniforms are good." This is the most common strategy.

In a technical challenge, the negative says that the case is a bad case. In other words, the case is too vague, not arguable, or not related to the resolution. This strategy is often difficult and boring, but if the affirmative makes a bad case, you must choose it.

In a countercase, the negative team says that the affirmative case is OK, but they have a better case. For example, if the affirmative case is "Our school should change its uniform to a green suit a tie," the negative team can countercase, "No, we should change our uniform to a brown suit and tie." Another possible countercase is, "No, we should have no uniforms at all."

In this chapter, we will study straight-out opposition, since it is the most popular strategy. A 1NC for straight-out opposition has 4 steps:

Step 1: Introduction
Step 2: Refutation of Affirmative Points
Step 3: 3-4 New Negative Points
Step 4: Conclusion

The 1NC points and conclusion are the same as for the 1AC (look again at page 41). During the introduction, you should thank the Speaker and the judge, paraphrase the affirmative case, and say that you disagree with it. Some 1NC's also like to tell a short story or joke during the introduction.

Refuting the affirmative points is very important. When you refute the other team's points, you explain why they do not prove the case. Six common refutations are: (a) the point is not true, (b) it is not **relevant**, (c) it is not **significant**, (d) it is **solvable**, (e) it **contradicts** other points, (f) it can be **flipped**.

Sometimes, a point is not true. For example, if the affirmative says that "Cats are noisier than dogs," the negative can say "No, they aren't. Dogs are often much noisier. For example..."

If a point is not relevant, the point may be true but does not prove the case. For example, if the case is "High school students should not wear uniforms," and the affirmative point is "Uniforms are ugly," then the negative can say, "Who cares? High school is about learning, not fashion. This point is not relevant."

If the point is not significant, the point is true, but only a little. For example, if the case is "Cats are better pets than dogs," and the affirmative point is "Cats are cheaper than dogs," than the negative can say, "Cats are only a little cheaper than dogs. The difference in cost is not significant."

Sometimes, a point is solvable without the case. For example, if the case is, "We should not import apples from other countries," and the affirmative makes the point that "foreign apples are not clean," then the negative may refute with "Yes, but apples are easy to wash, so there is no problem."

If 2 points disagree with each other, we say that they contradict. For example, if the case is "You should take your next trip to Canada," then two affirmative points may be that "You can practice your English," and "You can meet French people." These points contradict, since if you visit the French part of Canada, it will be difficult to practice English.

Sometimes you can change an affirmative point into a negative point. In other words, you can show that a point is true, relevant and significant, but it supports the negative side more than the affirmative side. The affirmative can do the same, and try to change a negative point into an affirmative point. This is called flipping the point. In debate, you should always try to flip the other team's points to your team. We will see some examples on the next page.

Questions:
1. **Why should you refute the affirmative's points before making your own points?**
2. **How much time should you spend on refutation and how much time on your own points?**

Task Chain

1. Kinds of Refutations

A. Read the points again on pages 32-33.

B. Read a 1NC's refutations of these points:

> The first point was "intelligence." We have 2 responses: First, cats are not smarter than dogs. How many cats help blind people? Second, intelligent pets are not always good pets. Many people enjoy pet fish, or pet mice, yet these are not smart animals.
>
> The second point was "noise." We have 3 responses: First, dogs are not always noisier than cats. I have been woken up many times by screaming cats. Second, dogs are easier to teach than cats. So if a dog is noisy, you can teach it to be quiet. Third, we think noisy pets are good pets, since they protect you better. A quiet cat will not scare away someone who is trying to steal your CD player.
>
> The third point was "cost." We have 3 responses: First, a small dog can eat less than a cat, so cats are not always cheaper than dogs. Second, cats usually eat less than dogs, but cat food is more expensive. Cats cost only a little less than dogs. Third, we think that expensive pets are often better than cheap pets. People usually protect expensive things more than cheap things. If you have an expensive pet, you will care about it more, and enjoy it more.

C. On page 49, we learned 6 ways to refute a point. How many of these ways are in part **B**.

2. Making Refutations

A. With a partner, read the 3 points on page 35. How can you refute these points? Write down as many refutations as you can.

B. Change partners, and give your refutations. Use these sentences:
Let me refute the _____ point. We have _____ responses.
First...... Second...... Third......

Flow other students' refutations.

C. Use your flows to repeat other students' refutations.

3. More Fighting Words

A. With a partner, match these words with their meaning. Use your dictionary.

1. get used to
2. atmosphere
3. destroy
4. equal
5. reject
6. bully
7. serious

A. kill / erase / break
B. have the same value
C. say "no"
D. force someone to do something
E. how most people feel in a place
F. important / likes to work hard
G. do something many times, so you don't hate it anymore

B. With a partner, derive new words. Use your dictionary. One word has 2 answers.

1. Something that hurts or kills is _____.
2. A _____ is a kind of warship.
3. A letter that says "no" is called a _____ letter.
4. In a democratic country, everyone has _____.
5. A large machine that digs and pushes the ground is a _____.

C. Which of these new words are nouns? verbs? adjectives?

D. Fill in the missing words in the conversation:

Pat: So, how do you like your new school?
Sebi: I love it. Everyone is very ¹·_____, but the ²·_____ is fun. The teachers give a lot of homework, but I've ³·_____ it.
Pat: Sounds great. I hate my new school. I didn't want to go there, but I was ⁴·_____ from everywhere else.
Sebi: What's the problem?
Pat: There are many ⁵·_____. They always take my money.
Sebi: That is a ⁶·_____ problem. You must tell your teacher. You are a new student, but still ⁷·_____ to everyone else.

4. Listening and Making Refutations

A. Listen again to the 1AC in **Chapter 5, Task Chain #6**, (page 44). Take a flow.

B. With a partner, think of good refutations for each point.

C. Change partners, and give your refutations to your new partner. Flow your new partner's refutations.

5. Flowing the 1NC

A. You should flow a 1NC next to the 1AC. You should write the refutations next to their points, and you should draw arrows. Look at the example.

1AC   **1NC**

[LINK]   [INTRODUCTION]

Case: Cats make better pets than dogs
   1: Intlgnce ———
     c. smarter d.   ————▶ — *not true: d. hp blind people*
     lost → *find home*   — *not relvt: not smart pets also good*
     vacatn → *leave food, cats save*   (for ex., fish, mice)
     d.: often lost, eat quickly
     smart → *easier/intrsting* → *better pets*
     d. → *circles 10 min* → *catch tail*

   2: Noise
     c. quieter d.   —
     d. noisy → *neighbors angry*   —
     c. quiet → *purr softly* → *good feeling* —
     d.: bark, bite
     quiet → *peaceful* → *better pets*
     woken up 3:00 a.m.

   3: cost
     c. cheaper care d.   —
     short vacation, pay for d. care   —
     c.: alone   —
     c. eat little; d., a lot
     cheaper pets → *save money* → *better*
     feed d. → *1000$ a year* → *fly Europe*

[CONCLUSION]   [NEGATIVE POINTS]
                                                      [CONCLUSION]

B. Using the refutations on page 50, write the missing points in the 1NC flow.

6. Listening and Flowing the 1NC

A. Write a new flow for the 1AC in **Chapter 5, Task Chain #6,** (page 44).

B. Now listen to a 1NC against the case. Flow the 1NC next to the 1AC.

C. Use your flow to repeat the 1NC.

MAKING IT HAPPEN

1. Application

Form groups of 3. The first student gives a 1AC. The other students flow, and prepare a 1NC. The second student gives the 1NC. Do this 3 times, changing roles.

2. Vocabulary Review

A. Look at the words below. Circle the words that you know.

strategy	*contradict*	*significant*
relevant	*solvable*	*difference*
refute	*rejection*	*refutation*
equality	*solution*	*relevance*
contradiction	*get used to*	*atmosphere*
destroy	*equal*	*reject*
bully	*serious*	*destructive*

B. Write a conversation with not more than 100 words. Use as many of these new words as you can.

C. Write down 7 more new words that you learned in this chapter. Write a definition for each word, and use each word in a sentence.

3. Questions for Discussion

A. On page 49, we studied six kinds of refutations. Can you think of any others?

B. What is the most difficult part of the 1NC speech? How can you make it easier?

7 Holistic Reasoning

FIGHTING WORDS

1. Words in Words

A. With a partner, match these words with their meanings. Use a dictionary.

1. deep
2. miss the point
3. logic
4. citizen
5. apply
6. heritage
7. key

A. art, culture, opinions, and so on, that come from the past
B. not simple/not easy to see or understand
C. very important
D. clear thinking, without emotion
E. take something and use it to do something else
F. a person who is a full member of a country
G. not understand the purpose of something

B. Which of these words are nouns? verbs? adjectives?

2. Words from Words

A. From the new words, derive adjectives. Use a dictionary.
1. An opinion with a clear reason is a _____ opinion.
2. Science that is used in everyday life is called _____ science.
3. Something that can be used is _____.
4. At a party, when many people give speeches, the most important speaker is the _____ speaker.

B. Now derive nouns from the new words. Again, use your dictionary.
1. A person who studies different ways of thinking is a _____.
2. All the people who live in a city or country are called the _____.
3. If you become a full member of a country, you take that country's _____.
4. If something can be used, it has an _____.

C. In English, when a word ends with "-ology," it means "study of." For example, zoology means "the study of animals." What do these words mean?
   1. astrology   2. sociology   3. biology
   4. geology   5. criminology   6. numerology

3. At a Loss for Words

Fill in the blanks with words from the last page.
Listen to the conversation to check your answers.

Lesson Focus

Read carefully, and answer the **Questions** at the end.

In debate, there are two kinds of reasoning, called **point-by-point reasoning** and **holistic reasoning**. In point-by-point reasoning, you prove or disprove the case with 3-4 different points. Your 3-4 different points are usually not related to each other. In holistic reasoning however, you don't make separate points. Instead, you connect your points together. You want to put your many different points into a **logical system**. You prove or disprove the case with this logical system.

Usually (but not always), we see mostly point-by-point reasoning early in the debate, and mostly holistic reasoning later in the debate. However, the best debaters will have some holistic reasoning in every speech, even the 1AC and 1NC.

To use holistic reasoning, there are 3 steps. First, you must ask the **key questions**. Second, you must answer the key questions. Finally, you must **apply** the answers to the case.

What are key questions? For example, let's look at the case "The government should give money to artists." Here, some key questions are:

1. Why do we have a government?
2. Why is art important?
3. What is art?

If you answer the key questions clearly, you will have a deeper understanding of the topic. In a debate, the team with the deeper understanding of the topic usually wins. If you can explain your deeper understanding to the judge, you will often win your debate.

Key questions help give you a deeper understanding of the topic, and help you explain it to the judge and audience. There are many kinds of key questions, but two kinds are most common. They are:

Definition Questions, such as, *What is art? What is education?*

Purpose Questions, such as, *Why do we have a government?*
Why do we have a judicial system?
Why do we have schools?

For example, look at the case "High school students should not study classical languages." A key question is "Why do people have to go to high school?"

There are many possible answers to this question. Here are four examples:

1. To learn useful information and skills for life
2. To learn how to think clearly and intelligently about many different subjects
3. To learn the country's heritage
4. To learn **morals** — in other words, to learn how to be a good person

In the debate, you should choose the answer or answers that support your opinion. For example, the negative team would probably like the third answer. They would explain their holistic reasoning like this:

> Mr. Speaker, the key question is, "Why do we have to go to high school?" There are many reasons, but one of the most important reasons is "to learn about our country's heritage." Why is it important to learn this? Our ancestors have left us a great heritage, and we dishonor them by forgetting it. Also, if we understand our heritage, we feel a closer relationship to our country and people. This makes us good citizens. Classical languages are an important part of our heritage. If we don't study them, we miss the point of high school.

If the negative team has time, they may choose other answers and apply them to the case.

Questions:

1. In the example, the negative asks a second key question. What is it? How many answers are there?

2. Look at the four answers to the question, "Why do people have to go to high school?" What answer would the affirmative team probably choose?

3. How about the other 2 answers? Which opinion do they support better — the affirmative or the negative?

Task Chain

1. Answering and Applying Key Questions

A. For the case "High school students should not wear uniforms," one key question is "How do students choose their clothes?" Two possible answers are:

1. They choose the best clothes to keep warm.
2. They choose the best clothes to look handsome or beautiful.

With a partner, write down 4 more answers.

B. Which answers support the affirmative? The negative? With your partner, decide which side your answers support, and why. Use sentences like these:

I think "to keep warm" supports the affirmative. If students are too cold, they can get sick and miss school. This is bad for students.

I think "to look handsome or beautiful" supports the negative. School is about learning, not fashion. Students should not worry about such things in school.

2. Choosing, Answering and Applying Key Questions

A. Now look at the case "Dogs make better pets than cats." Which is the best key question? Look at these 4 questions, and choose the best key question.

1. What are dogs?
2. What are pets?
3. Why do people keep pets?
4. How much does dog food cost?

B. Now, with a partner, write down 5 possible answers to the key question.

C. Which answers support the affirmative? The negative? With your partner, decide which side your answers support, and why.

D. Change partners. Explain your holistic reasoning to your new partner. First, explain an affirmative answer, then a negative answer. Flow your new partner's holistic reasoning.

E. Use your flow to repeat your new partner's holistic reasoning.

3. More Fighting Words

A. With a partner, match these words with their meanings. Use a dictionary.

1. moral agent
2. human rights
3. reduce
4. violate
5. make sure
6. deserve
7. veto

A. should have / should be given
B. break / hurt / not keep a promise
C. check very carefully
D. cancel
E. for example, freedom of speech or freedom of religion
F. make fewer / make less
G. a living thing that understands the difference between good and evil

B. Look up the words *reduce*, *violate*, and *moral* in your dictionary. What words can you derive from them?

4. Answering Difficult Key Questions

A. Many key questions are very difficult to answer. For example, "What is justice?" "Why do we have a government?" "What are human rights?" "Why do we have human rights?" If you have a difficult key question, and you need a hint, you can use conditional sentences. Please review conditional sentences on page 20.

B. For example, if the question is "Why do we have a government?" you can make sentences like:
If there were no government, there would be no police to protect us.
If there were no government, all schools would be private, and only rich children would be able to go to school.

With a partner, make 5 more sentences like this about the government.

C. In groups of 4, write down at least 3 conditional sentences related to the following questions. When you are finished, think of an answer for each question. Compare your answers with other groups.

1. What are human rights?
2. Why do people believe in religion?
3. Why is art important?
4. What is culture?
5. Why do we have a justice system?

5. Some Common Key Questions

A. Read these questions:
   1. What are human rights?
   2. Why do people believe in religion?
   3. Where do human rights come from?
   4. Why do we have governments?

B. Now read these answers. In groups of four, match the answers with the question. Each question has at least 2 answers.

Use sentences like this:
> *I think "in order to protect each person's freedom" answers the question "Why do we have government?"*
> *I think so too. / I don't think so.*

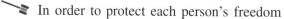 In order to protect each person's freedom
1. Because people want to understand the world, and it answers many questions
2. Because people want a relationship with God
3. Rules about how government should treat people
4. Personal vetos over laws that reduce freedom
5. They are given by God to people
6. We are born with them; we have them because we are moral agents
7. Freedoms that every person needs to live a happy life
8. When people make governments, they decide together to have them
9. In order to make a happier, richer country
10. In order to protect equality, to make sure that everyone can try to be happy

6. Listening to Holistic Reasoning

Listen to John and Mary. They are debating the case that "The government should give money to the arts."

A. Who is on the affirmative? Who is on the negative?

B. Listen again, and flow their speeches.

MAKING IT HAPPEN

1. Application

A. With a partner, choose any cases that you have studied before. Write the holistic reasoning.

B. Listen to other students read their case and holistic reasoning. Take a flow. Use your flow to repeat other students' holistic reasoning.

C. Now prepare the holistic reasoning for another 2 cases, but do not write down every word. Instead, write a flow for your own speech.

D. Listen to other students explain, from their notes, their cases and holistic reasoning. Take a flow. Use your flow to repeat other students' holistic reasoning.

2. Vocabulary Review

A. Look at the words and expressions below. Circle the ones that you know.

deep	miss the point	logic
citizen	apply	heritage
key	keynote	logical
applied	applicable	citizenship
citizenry	logician	veto
human rights	reduce	violate
make sure	deserve	moral agent

B. Put these words into groups of 4-7 words. You may make any group that will help you remember the words. Compare your groups with a partner.

C. Write down 7 more new words that you learned in this chapter. Write a conversation with the 7 new words.

3. Questions for Discussion

A. Which do you think is stronger — point by point reasoning or holistic reasoning? Why?

B. Which do you think is easier? Why?

8 Members' Speeches

FIGHTING WORDS

1. Words in Words

A. With a partner, match these words with their meaning. Use your dictionary.

1. organize   A. can say many things with few words
2. concise   B. forget about / stop talking about / stop doing
3. set   C. start talking about
4. reaffirm   D. say again / explain again
5. responsibility   E. put things in a neat order / make a clear system
6. drop   F. decided before / always the same
7. introduce   G. something that you must do

B. Which of these words are nouns? verbs? adjectives?

2. Words from Words

A. From the new words, derive adjectives. Use a dictionary.
   1. A person who always does what he or she has to do is a _____ person.
   2. A person who keeps things in a neat system is an _____ person.
   3. Something that has been decided is _____.

B. From the new words, derive nouns. Again, use your dictionary.
   1. The person who manages an event is the _____.
   2. A group which does things together is called an _____.
   3. A person who quits school before finishing is a _____.
   4. If you promise something for a second time, you make a _____.

C. In English, we sometimes add letters to the beginning of a word. By adding letters, we can change a word into its opposite. In your dictionary, look for words that begin with **ir-**, **dis-**, **in-**, or **un-**, and make new words:
   1. A person who doesn't keep things neatly is a _____ person.
   2. A person who doesn't do what he has to do is an _____ person.
   3. Something that has not been decided yet is _____.

3. At a Loss for Words

Fill in the blanks with words from the last page.
Listen to the conversation to check your answers.

lesson focus

Read carefully, and answer the **Questions**.

The speeches after the 1NC are called the **Second Affirmative Constructive** (2AC) and the **Second Negative Constructive** (2NC). If the debate has 3-person teams, the 2NC is followed by a 3AC and a 3NC. The 2AC, 2NC, 3AC and 3NC are all called **members' speeches**, while the 1AC and the 1NC are called **leaders' speeches**.

Members' speeches do not have set steps. In other words, members' speeches do not all have the same "Step 1," "Step 2," "Step 3" and so on. There are many different ways to organize a member's speech. However, each speech has special responsibilities.

The 2AC has 4 responsibilities:

1. The 2AC must refute all the 1NC points. This is very important. **Dropping** points is very dangerous.

2. The 2AC must reaffirm the important 1AC points. The 1NC should have refuted all of the 1AC points. The 2AC must respond to these refutations. If the 1NC dropped an affirmative point, then the 2AC should say to the judge, "The negative team dropped the point about…"

3. The 2AC should make some new points to support the case. This is especially important when each team has 3 people.

4. The 2AC should introduce the affirmative's holistic reasoning. This is especially important when each team has 2 people.

5. The 2AC should **impact dropped points**. If the 1NC dropped points, these points should be explained again with strong impacts. The 2AC should also use these points in its holistic reasoning.

There are different rules about new points in the 2AC. In the US and Canada, the most important affirmative points are in the 1AC. New points in the 2AC are usually not very strong. However, in Australia, the UK and Ireland, the affirmative gives half of its strongest points to the 1AC, and half to the 2AC.

The 2NC's responsibilities are similar to the 2AC's, but the 2NC has more freedom. Some 2NC's spend 80% of their time on holistic reasoning. Other 2NC's make new points as quickly as they can — a fast 2NC can make over 10 points in 5 minutes. Most 2NC's are in the middle; they spend some time on holistic reasoning, some time on new points, and some time on old points. The 2NC's most important responsibility, though, is to refute all new points made by the 2AC.

Debate teams usually have 2 people. However, in Australia and Southeast Asia, 3-person teams are more popular. The 3AC and 3NC speeches are called **summation** speeches, or **summary** speeches. **Summarize** means "explain again the most important facts concisely." During a summation, you should explain what the most important points have been, and why your side's points have been better than the other team's.

In a summation, a debater must not make new points. If you make new points in summation, judges will usually not listen to them, and they will give your team a penalty. However, you can explain old points in new ways, with new examples and new impacts.

In a summation, it is very important to compare your team's points with the other team's points. Many 3AC and 3NC's forget to do this; they only repeat their teammates' points. Such speeches are weak and boring. Sometimes, the 3AC and the 3NC are the last speeches of the debate. They should be as strong and interesting as possible.

In England, Scotland and Ireland, debate teams usually have 4 people. In this case, the 3AC and the 3NC have the same responsibilities as the 2AC and the 2NC. The 4AC and the 4NC are summation speeches, and they are always the last speeches of the debate.

Like all speeches, member speeches should thank the Speaker, and end with a conclusion. Many debaters like to begin their speeches with a short story, in order to relax the judge.

Questions:
As for new points in the 2AC, who has the better system – North America or Australia? Why?

Task Chain

1. Reading a 2AC

A. Listen again to the 1AC and 1NC's on the resolution, "Students should have more freedom," in **Chapter 5, Task Chain #6**, (page 44) and **Chapter 6, Task Chain #5**, (page 52). Flow them next to each other.

B. Now read this 2AC for the same debate. Flow this speech next to the 1NC. Draw arrows between the points.

> Thank you Mr. Speaker, ladies and gentlemen. To support the case that "High school students should not wear uniforms," I will do 3 things. First, I will reaffirm my partner's points. Second, I will refute the negative points. Finally, I will make a new affirmative point.
>
> First, I will reaffirm my partner's points. On the point of comfort, the negative team has responded that (a) uniforms are comfortable, and (b) students should not be comfortable in school. These two refutations contradict each other, and are both wrong. Uniforms are not comfortable. If they were comfortable, students would wear them in their free time. Also, students should be comfortable in school. When students study at home, they usually wear casual clothes. If you are relaxed, you study better.
>
> On the point of the real world. School is about more than English and math — it's a place where students learn how to live in society. Of course, people sometimes wear uniforms to their jobs. However, choosing clothes is still a key part of life, and should be a part of the education experience as well.
>
> On the point of personal expression, clothes are a very important part of personal expression, even more than speaking or writing. Not everyone hears what you say, or reads what you write, but everyone sees how you dress. Yes, people often choose the same clothes as their friends, but that's how people express their friendship and respect. There is nothing destructive about casual clothes. They are a large part of our culture, and there is no reason to keep them out of school.
>
> Now, I will refute the 1NC's points. Her first point was "serious atmosphere." We have 2 responses. First, you can have a serious atmosphere without uniforms. Most universities don't have uniforms, but are still very serious.
> Second, uniforms do not make a serious atmosphere. There are many students who wear uniforms, but don't study or take school seriously.

Her second point was "equality." I'll refute this point in 2 ways. First, when students wear uniforms, rich students will wear expensive rings, or have expensive gadgets, or ride expensive bicycles. Rich students will always show their wealth, and poorer students will feel that they need more money. Abolishing uniforms does not change this. Second, in the real world, there are richer people and poorer people. Students have to learn how to relate with people richer and poorer than them. Schools should teach reality, not hide from it.

Her third point was "bullying." This point really supports our side. Students bully students who are different from them. Uniforms strengthen this way of thinking. When everyone wears uniforms, students get the message that "Everyone should be the same." When everyone wears different clothes, students get the message that "It's OK to be different." Yes, many students have committed suicide because of bullying, but how many of them came from schools with uniforms?

Now, I'd like to add one new point: "the economy." Clothing is a very important business, and thousands of people work in the clothing industry. If students stop wearing uniforms, they will buy more casual clothing. This will make a lot of new business for clothing makers and clothing stores. Thousands of men and women in our country want to work, but can't find jobs. By abolishing uniforms, we can put many of these people back to work, and make our country stronger.

Mr. Speaker, we have proven our case on four main points: comfort, the real world, personal expression, and the economy. The negative points have all been insignificant, or completely wrong. For these reasons, we beg to propose.

C. Are there any problems with this 2AC? Look again at the responsibilities of a 2AC on page 64. Have they all been done in this speech?

2. Listening to 2AC's

A. Take a very large sheet of paper and make 6 columns. In the first column, flow the 1AC in **Chapter 5, Task Chain #6**, (page 44). In the second column flow the 1NC in **Chapter 6, Task Chain #6**, (page 52).

B. Listen to two more 2AC's, and flow them in the third and fourth columns.

C. Look again at the 2AC's responsibilities. Are there any problems with these 2AC's?

3. Listening to 2NC's

A. Listen to two 2NC's, and flow them in the fifth and sixth columns from the previous exercise.

B. Look again at the responsibilities of a 2NC on page 64. Are there any problems with these 2NC's?

4. What are the Problems?

In this chapter, we have flowed 5 members' speeches (3 2AC's and 2 2NC's). Each speech had some problems. Match the five speeches with the correct description below.

A. This speech has some very good reasoning, but it is very **disorganized**. In other words, the debater talks about many things, but there is no logical order. This speech is difficult to flow and difficult to listen to.

B. This speech is not bad. It discusses all the points of the debate, and introduces new reasoning. However, there is no holistic reasoning, no summary, and no direct comparison with the other team. It also spends too much time on old points and not enough on new ones. It is an OK speech, but it adds only a little to the debate.

C. This speech has a lot of good reasoning, however, it does not talk at all about the other team's points. It drops everything the other team said. This makes a poor debate. It is a weak strategy for the affirmative, and a no-win strategy for the negative.

D. This speech has the opposite problem as **C** — it talks only about the other team's points. It drops everything the first speaker on the team said, and does not make any new points. It refutes the other team very well, but doesn't prove its own side. This is a weak strategy for the negative, and a no-win strategy for the affirmative.

E. This speech has a lot of interesting ideas, but doesn't talk about school uniforms. It is not relevant, and therefore a poor speech for this debate.

Making It Happen

1. Application

Form groups of 6 or 8. Choose any of the resolutions that we have studied, and hold a debate. Use teams of 3 or 4 people. The last two member speeches will be the last speeches of the debate, so they will be summary speeches. Speeches should last 3 or 4 minutes, with 1 or 2 minutes preparation time between speeches.

2. Vocabulary Review

A. Look at the words below. Circle the words that you know.

organize	*introduce*	*irresponsible*
drop	*concise*	*unorganized*
responsibility	*settled*	*disorganized*
set	*reaffirm*	*organization*
unsettled	*organizer*	*dropout*
disorganized	*gadget*	*reaffirmation*

B. Have a 2-minute conversation with your partner. How many of these new words can you use?

C. Write down 7 more new words that you learned in this chapter. Write a story with the 7 new words.

3. Questions for Discussion

A. Do you prefer teams of 3 people or 4 people? Why?

B. Dropping the other team's points is always bad, but it is much worse for the negative. Dropping your partner's points is always bad, but it is much worse for the affirmative. Why?

9 Rebuttals and Judging

FIGHTING WORDS

1. Words in Words

A. With a partner, match these words with their meanings. Use your dictionary.

1. advantage
2. consecutive
3. explicit
4. basic
5. burden
6. clash
7. fulfill

A. one right after another
B. responsibility
C. something that helps you
D. do / finish
E. first / most important
F. fight / oppose
G. very clear

B. Which words are nouns? verbs? adjectives?

C. What's the difference between *burden* and *responsibility*?

2. Words from Words

A. From the new words, derive adjectives. Use your dictionary.
1. Something that helps you is _____.
2. Something that is very difficult is _____.
3. If you have finished something difficult, and are happy, you feel _____.
4. Someone who has a big problem, and is worrying, is _____.
5. Something that makes you feel useful is _____.

B. Make opposites. Look in your dictionary under **dis-**, **in-**, **non-**, or **un-**.
1. Something that hurts you is _____.
2. When you tell someone your problems, you _____ yourself.
3. When you stop doing something, but you don't feel happy, you are _____.
4. Something that is not clear is _____.

C. How many of the new words can be derived into adverbs? Look for the abbreviation "adv." in your dictionary.

3. At a Loss for Words

Fill in the blanks with words from the last page.
Listen to the conversation to check your answers.

lesson focus

Read carefully, and answer the **Questions**.

In some debates, the 3NC or the 4NC is the last speech. Usually, however, there are special speeches after the constructives. These are called the **rebuttal speeches** or **reply speeches**. Usually, each team has one rebuttal. These rebuttals are called the **negative rebuttal**, or NR, and the **affirmative rebuttal**, or the AR.

The negative team always gives the first rebuttal. Therefore, the negative team has 2 consecutive speeches (2NC - 1NR). This time is called the **negative bloc**. If the negative gives a lot of information during these two speeches, it is difficult for the affirmative to respond to all of it. This is a big **advantage** for the negative.

However, because the negative gives the first rebuttal, the affirmative team speaks last in the debate. The affirmative can make the last refutations, and the last impacts. This is a big advantage for the affirmative team. The negative bloc and the speaking-last advantages are about equal, so they are balanced.

In a rebuttal, you have two responsibilities. First, you must summarize the debate, especially the holistic reasoning. We studied summaries on page 65. Second, you must explain why you have won the debate.

Usually, a rebuttal takes half the time of a constructive. For example, if each constructive speech is 6 minutes, rebuttals will usually be 3 minutes. Because rebuttals are short, you must be very concise. It is impossible to discuss every point of the debate, so you must choose only the important points that make you win.

In the rebuttal, you may not make new points. If you do, the judges will not listen and will give your team a penalty. In some debate rules, if you make new arguments, the other team may stop your speech and complain to the judge. This is called a **point of order**. Points of order are very common in American debates.

Sometimes, if there are 2-person teams, both debaters give a rebuttal. These rebuttals are called the **first negative rebuttal**, **first affirmative rebuttal**, **second negative rebuttal** and **second affirmative rebuttal**. We can abbreviate these speeches as 1NR, 1AR, 2NR and 2AR.

In your rebuttal, you must explain to the judge why you have won the debate. But how do teams win debates? How does a judge decide who has won?

First, we have **basic burdens**. The affirmative has 2 basic burdens; the negative team has 1. If a team does not fulfill its burdens, it loses the debate.

The affirmative burdens are: (a) to make a clear, debatable case from the resolution; and (b) to prove its case. These are called the **burden of definition** and the **burden of proof**. The negative burden is to find problems with the affirmative case and reasoning. This is called the **burden of clash**. In other words, if the affirmative team does not propose a clear, debatable case, it loses the debate. If the affirmative team proposes a good case, but gives irrelevant and insignificant points, it loses the debate. If the negative team does not talk about the affirmative case and reasoning, then it loses the debate.

How else can teams lose debates? There are many ways, for example:

— The other team does not refute your most important points.
— The other team contradicts itself.
— The other team's points are not clear.
— The other team's points are not strong, and are all refuted.
— Your points are stronger than the other team's points.
— Your holistic reasoning is stronger than the other team's.

In your rebuttal, you should say explicitly to the judge, "We have won this debate because...," or "They have lost this debate because..."

Questions:

1. How else can teams lose a debate? Write down 3 more reasons.

2. The affirmative has two basic burdens; the negative has one. Is this an advantage to the negative? What advantage does the affirmative have to balance it?

Task Chain

1. Negative Rebuttal

A. Flow four constructive speeches on the topic "Students should have more freedom." Use the 1AC on page 44, **#6**; the 1NC on page 52, **#6**; the 2AC on page 67, **#2 A-1**; and the 2NC on page 68, **#3 A-1**.

B. Read this NR, and flow it next to the 2NC.

> Mr. Speaker, ladies and gentlemen. In this debate, the affirmative team took the resolution that "Students should have more freedom," and proposed the case "High school students should not wear uniforms." To support this case, they talked about comfort, the real world and personal expression.
>
> In my first speech, Mr. Speaker, I refuted all these points. I explained why uniforms are comfortable. I explained why "the real world" point was not relevant or significant. I explained how students can have personal expression without uniforms. But the 2AC did not respond to these refutations. The 2AC dropped all of our responses. She repeated her partner's points, but she didn't explain why our refutations were wrong. The affirmative points have all fallen.
>
> Similarly, my partner and I have made many negative arguments. We talked about a serious atmosphere. Please remember my partner's example — would you go to a wedding in jeans and a T-shirt? The affirmative team has not answered this point. We talked about equality. Please remember my partner's story about his high school days. The affirmative team never answered this point. We talked about bullying — a very serious problem, with students committing suicide. But the affirmative team didn't talk about this either.
>
> Mr. Speaker, ladies and gentlemen. The affirmative team has lost this debate, because they have not supported their own points, and they have dropped everything that we have said. I ask you to vote to keep uniforms, and to help make schools safe, serious, and equal for all.

C. Are there any problems with this NR? Look again at the responsibilities of an NR on page 72. Have they all been done in this speech?

2. Affirmative Rebuttal

A. Read this AR, and flow it next to the NR from page 74.

> Mr. Speaker, Ladies and Gentlemen. From the resolution "Students should have more freedom," we proposed the case that high school students should not wear uniforms. In my speech, I made three points. My partner reaffirmed these points, and added one more.
>
> My first point was "comfort." Both my partner and I explained that some students get hot very easily, and some get cold very easily. But everyone wears the same uniform, so some students are too hot or too cold. The negative team said that students can wear T-shirts or open their collars, but can they always do this? We don't think so. Comfortable students enjoy school more, and learn more, which is why we should abolish uniforms.
>
> My second point was "the real world." School is where we learn important skills for the real world. Isn't wearing clothes important? Why should students wear uniforms that they will never wear again when they finish school? Uniforms have no relation to reality, so they should not be a part of school.
>
> My third point was "personal expression." My partner explained that in school, we want to make people, not robots. We want students to learn how to express themselves. When students choose their own clothes, they are expressing themselves to the world. This is a very important part of our school system.
>
> Finally, my partner made the point of "confidence." Because students choose clothes that look nice, they become more confident. Confident students like to express themselves, enjoy working in groups, and often try new things. Confident students are better students, so we should abolish uniforms.
>
> For all these reasons, it is clear that uniforms make poor schools. We ask you to vote with our side, and make schools more interesting and relevant to students.

B. Are there any problems with this AR?

C. Who has won the debate? Why?

3. Listening to Rebuttals

A. Listen to another NR, and take a flow.

B. Listen to another AR, and take a flow.

C. Are there any problems with these rebuttals?

4. What are the Problems?

In this chapter, we have flowed 4 rebuttals (2 NR's and 2 AR's). Match the four speeches with the correct description below.

A. This rebuttal is like a mini-constructive. It only paraphrases the team's points. It never compares the two sides, and it does not explain why the other team has lost.

B. This is a good rebuttal, even though it could use some holistic reasoning. Holistic reasoning has been weak the entire debate.

C. This speech talks only about the other team's points; it never reaffirms its own points, and it does not explain why it has won the debate. It also has a lot of new reasoning. This is not a strong rebuttal.

D. In this rebuttal, the debater speaks quickly, and tries to talk about every point in the debate. The debater is not concise at all. There is also no summary. This kind of speech is called a **trench-warfare rebuttal**, and is weak.

5. Making Rebuttals

A. Flow four constructive speeches on the topic "Students should have more freedom." Use the 1AC on page 44, **#6**; the 1NC on page 51, **#6**; the 2AC on page 67, **#2 A-2**; and the 1NC on page 68, **#3 A-2**.

B. Write an NR and AR for each side.

C. Listen to other students make their NR's and AR's. Flow them. Are there any problems?

MAKING IT HAPPEN

1. Application

You can now have full debates. Choose any topic (there are example topics on pages 86 and 87). Make teams of 2 or 3. This first speaker for each team will also give a rebuttal. You may choose how long each speech will be, but constructive speeches should last 4-7 minutes, and rebuttals will last 2-4.

For preparation time, you may give 1-2 minutes between each team's speeches for preparation. (Do not give a break between the last negative constructive and the negative rebuttal.) Or, you may give each team 4-5 minutes, which it may use whenever it wants.

2. Vocabulary Review

A. Look at the words below. Circle the words that you know.

advantage	*fulfill*	basic
explicit	*non-consecutive*	*advantageous*
unburden	*clash*	*consecutive*
fulfilling	*inexplicit*	*burden*
burdensome	*disadvantageous*	*unfulfilled*

B. Write a story with all these new words.

C. Write down 5 new words that you learned in this chapter. Write a definition for each word.

3. Questions for Discussion

A. When you have rebuttals, do you prefer teams of 2 or 3 people? Why?

B. Are rebuttals easier or harder than constructives? Why?

C. In Canadian debate, only the affirmative gets a rebuttal (usually 3 minutes). To balance this, the last negative constructive is 3 minutes longer than the other constructives. There is no special "negative rebuttal" speech. What are the good points and bad points of this system?

10 Style

FIGHTING WORDS

1. Words in Words

A. With a partner, match these words with their meanings. Use your dictionary.

1. substance
2. include
3. confused
4. persuade
5. gesture
6. confident
7. monotonous

A. boring, because it is always the same
B. can't understand / don't know what to do
C. make someone agree with you
D. material / what is inside something else
E. brave / when you feel that you will do well
F. have inside
G. move your hands when you speak

B. Which words are nouns? verbs? adjectives? One word has two answers.

2. Words from Words

A. From the new words, derive nouns. Use your dictionary.
1. A voice with no melody is a _____.
2. When your life is never exciting, you have _____.
3. A situation when nobody knows what to do is called _____.
4. If you feel that you will succeed, you have _____.

B. From the new words, derive adjectives. Again, use your dictionary.
1. Something that is very large is _____ or _____.
2. A person who can change other people's opinions is _____.
3. A club with many kinds of people is an _____ club.
4. If you don't understand something, it is _____.

C. Look at the word "monotonous." The first four letters, "mono-," mean "one." Many words begin with "mono-." Use your dictionary, and find these words:
1. A person who has only one wife is a _____.
2. Something with only one color is _____.
3. A person who believes in only one God is a _____.
4. If something has only one language, it is _____.

3. At a Loss for Words

Fill in the blanks with words from the last page.
Listen to the conversation to check your answers.

Lesson focus

Read carefully, and answer the **Questions**.

In a debate, your **substance** is very important. Substance means "what you say." To win a debate, you must have good points, logic, refutation, examples, organization, and so on. Substance is also called **matter**. **Style** is also very important in a debate. Style means "how you speak." It includes your body language and voice. Style is also called **manner**.

Body language is very important in debate. You should always look **confident**. If you do not look confident, the judge will think, "Why is the debater so nervous? Doesn't she believe what she is saying? If she doesn't believe her own speech, maybe I shouldn't believe it either." But if you look confident, the judge will think, "Wow! This debater really believes what she's saying. Maybe I should believe it too." In other words, if you are more confident, you will be more **persuasive**.

Question 1

When you are nervous, what does your body do? How about when you are confident?

Here are a few hints for good body language:

1. You should look usually at the judge, occasionally at the audience, and rarely at your notes. Never look at the floor, the ceiling, the windows, the door and so on.

2. When you are not gesturing, rest your hands at the sides of your body. Do not lean on your desk, play with your pen or notebook, put your hands in your pockets or on your head, or hold your hands together in front of your body.

3. Balance on both feet, and do not walk too much. You should walk a little between points, but you should usually not walk during a point. However, sometimes, you can walk toward the judge during an impact. This makes the impact look more important.

4. Use your hands and your face to show your emotions when you speak. For example, you may smile when making a funny point, or you may bang the table when you are angry.

Your voice is also very important. You should not speak in a **monotone**; in other words, you should always change the **speed**, **volume** and **pitch** of your voice. Speed means "how fast you speak"; it can be either faster or slower. Volume means "how loud you speak"; it can be either louder or softer. Pitch means "how high you speak," for example, violins are higher than cellos. Pitch can be either higher or lower.

In English, we use speed, volume and pitch to show emotion. If you speak in a monotone, your speech will seem very boring, and the judge and audience will not be interested. You should use your voice to show emotion in your speech. For example, if you are being funny, you may speak a little faster and higher. If you are sad, you may speak softer, slower and lower.

Question 2
How do your volume, pitch, and speed change when you are serious? angry? happy? excited? relaxed?

Here are a few hints for good voice:

1. You should not speak too quietly. It is important that everyone in the room hear you. Imagine your voice coming from deep down inside your body, not from your throat. This will make your voice stronger.

2. You should stress the important words in each sentence. This helps the judge and other team understand what you are saying.

3. If you don't know what to say, you should pause for a second. Don't say words like *aaaahhhhh, errrrr, eeeeeeeh, ummmmmm*. When you say these words, the judge thinks, "This debater is confused. If he doesn't understand this case, why should I listen to him?"

4. When you begin a point, you should speak at average speed and volume. As you explain your point, you can slowly become faster, slower, louder or softer. Your impact should be the fastest, slowest, loudest or softest part of the point. You should pause for a moment between points, and start your next point at average speed and volume.

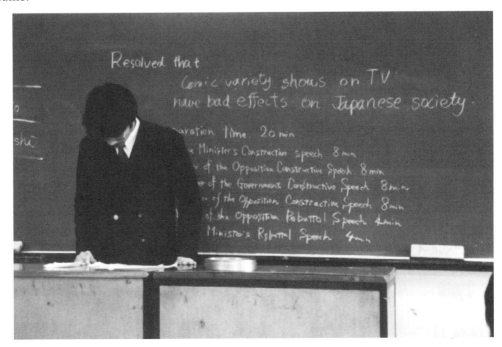

Task Chain

1. Body Language

A. Look at these pictures. What's wrong with these debaters' body language?

B. Look at these debaters' gestures and faces. What are they talking about? Use your imagination.

2. Stressing Important Words

A. In English, we stress the important words in every sentence. Sometimes, the stressed words are new information. For example, look at this conversation:

John: Which car is yours?
Mary: The **yellow** one.

Mary stresses "yellow" because it is new information.

B. When you stress a word, you say it a little louder and higher. (If you are angry or serious, you say it a little louder and lower.) Listen, and practice this conversation:

John: So, what did you **do** last Saturday?
Mary: I went **shopping**.
John: Where?
Mary: I went to the **new** store **downtown**.
John: **What** did you **buy**?
Mary: I bought a **dress** and a **jacket**.
John: What **color** jacket?
Mary: It was **red** and **yellow.**

C. Other times, we stress information that shows what we are thinking. For example, look at this picture:

John says "I love you," but he stresses different words in different situations. Read these situations, and choose which word to stress.

1. John loves Mary, but Mary thinks John loves other women. John is thinking, "I love only you, Mary."
2. John loves Mary, but Mary loves Mike. Mike doesn't love Mary. John is thinking, "Mike doesn't love you. I love you. Please love me too."
3. John loves Mary very much, but Mary doesn't know. Before now, John and Mary were just friends. John is thinking, "I don't just like you, I love you!"

3. Listening for Stress

A. Listen to 5 speakers say "Mr. Smith was a math teacher." Which word do they stress? Write the stressed word below. The first one is done for you.

1. _was_   2. _____   3. _____   4. _____   5. _____

B. What are the speakers thinking in each situation? Use your imagination.

1. *Mr. Smith was a math teacher two years ago, but now he's retired.*
2. _____
3. _____
4. _____
5. _____

C. To a partner, say "Mr. Smith was a math teacher." Choose any word and stress it. Can your partner hear the stressed word?

4. Making Quotations

A. When we quote something in English, we pause before and after the quotation. We also change our pitch. Your pitch can be either higher or lower, but it must be different. Listen and practice:

1. The teacher said, "Sit down, and listen to me!"
2. "Sit down, and listen to me!" the teacher said.
3. "Sit down," the teacher said, "and listen to me!"

B. What is your favorite quotation? In groups of 4, tell your group your favorite quotation and explain what it means. For example:

Martin Luther King said, "We cannot take the tranquilizing drug of gradualism." It means that if you have a big problem, you should fix it quickly. If you say, "I'll fix it a little bit now, and finish it later," you will forget about it.

5. Listening for Good Voice

A. Read the "intelligence" point on page 32.

B. Now listen to 3 debaters make the "intelligence" point. How are their voices? What are the problems with each debater's voice?

MAKING IT HAPPEN

1. Application

A. **Charade game**. Make teams of 4 or 5. Each team chooses a captain. The teacher gives each captain a word or title. The captain uses gestures and body language to tell the team what the word or title is. The first team to guess the word or title gets a point. Change captains after every word. The captain can only use body language — no talking.

B. **Style drills**. Form groups of 4. Prepare a 3-minute speech on any topic. You don't have to write every word when you prepare. Make your speech to your group, and watch other speeches. For each speech, write down good points and bad points about the body language and voice.

2. Vocabulary Review

A. Look at the words below. Circle the words that you know.

monotonous	*confidence*	*persuasive*
gesture	*monotony*	*substantial*
confusing	*inclusive*	*monotone*
substance	*confusion*	*confident*
include	*substantive*	*confused*

B. Put these words in 3 groups. Make any groups that will help you remember the words. Compare your groups with a partner.

C. Write down 7 new words that you learned in this chapter. Compare your new words with a partner. Have a 2-minute conversation with your partner. Use as many new words as you can.

3. Questions for Discussion

A. In a debate, which do you think is more important — style or substance? Which is easier?

B. What are some common gestures in your country? Do people in English-speaking countries use the same gestures?

C. Why do debaters use quotations?

Some Resolutions for Debate

Animals
Resolved: We should not wear fur.
Resolved: The government should protect farm animals more.
Resolved: The government should do more to protect endangered species.
Resolved: It's more important to create jobs than save endangered species.
Resolved: Cosmetic / scientific testing on animals should be banned.

Charity
Resolved: We should give money to beggars.
Resolved: Rich countries should increase aid to poor countries.
Resolved: The government should help poor people more.
Resolved: Rich countries should not tell poor countries how to use aid money.

Diversity / Internationalism
Resolved: It should be easier / harder to come to live in this country.
Resolved: It should be easier / harder to become a citizen of this country.
Resolved: Companies should make great effort to hire more minorities.
Resolved: Diverse countries are better than homogeneous countries.
Resolved: A world government is inevitable / desirable.

Education
Resolved: Single-sex schools are better than co-ed schools.
Resolved: The school year should begin in _____.
Resolved: Students should / should not have to study _____.
Resolved: Strong students and weak students should have different classes.
Resolved: Students should / should not be allowed to _____.
Resolved: Entrance examinations should be abolished.
Resolved: Students should be separated into academic or vocational schools at an early age.

The Environment
Resolved: We should promote recycling / new kinds of energy.
Resolved: Cars should be banned / restricted.
Resolved: Nuclear power should be abolished.
Resolved: The rain forest should be protected.

Family

Resolved: Arranged marriages are better than love-based marriages.
Resolved: It's better to be married than single.
Resolved: Divorce should be easier / harder to get.
Resolved: It's better to live with your extended family than your nuclear family.
Resolved: Family is more valuable than friends.
Resolved: Gay and Lesbian marriage should be allowed.

Law and Politics

Resolved: It's better to have a king than a president.
Resolved: Voting should be compulsory.
Resolved: Capital / corporal punishment should be abolished / restored.

Medicine

Resolved: People should have the right to die.
Resolved: Doctors should tell patients when they have an incurable disease.

Religion

Resolved: We should believe in God.
Resolved: Religion has done more harm than good to human society.
Resolved: Reincarnation is better than going directly to heaven or hell.

Travel

Resolved: We should take our next vacation in _____.
Resolved: Mountain vacations are better than sea vacations.
Resolved: Foreign vacations are better than domestic vacations.
Resolved: We should visit poor countries rather than rich ones.
Resolved: It's better to live and work in a country than to visit it as a tourist.

Women's Issues

Resolved: It's better to be a woman than a man.
Resolved: The government should force companies to hire more women.
Resolved: Women and men should pay equally on dates.
Resolved: One-third of all seats in the legislature should be reserved for women.

Acknowledgments

Many people played crucial roles in the evolution of this book. First and foremost, I must thank Michael S. Carroll, my friend and colleague at Sagami Women's University High School. It was originally his idea to synthesize explicit ESL/EFL targets with debate material. He was also one of the primary testers of the material in his Oral Communication class, and has made many important comments.

Shari J. Berman and Alice L. Bratton of Harcourt Brace Japan have been equally essential to the production of this text. In addition to tirelessly managing the innumerable tasks on the publishing side, they gave me an extensive education in how to turn a pile of ideas into a proper textbook. I am especially grateful for all their time and dedication to seeing this work succeed.

For the beautiful artwork, I must thank Yoko Hama, Chino Hirabayashi, Akiko Ogata, Ayako Tokunaga, Mariko Mozawa and Risa Tsuyuki of the Sagami Women's University High School Manga Club, and their faculty advisor, Kyoko Kusano. For the excellent photos, I must thank Makiko Suzuki and the illustrious Cteavin Santos, as well as the organizers of the 17th World Universities Debating Championships and the 13th Kanto Universities ESS League Parliamentary Debate Tournament.

I am grateful to Amy D. Yamashiro and John William McLaughlin, who read through the early version and suggested many important changes. I am very much indebted to Professor Alan Cirlin of St. Mary's University for his extensive critique and commentary.

Thanks also to Joseph Dilenscheider and Stephen Brivati for their comments for the revised edition.

Special thanks to the 1996–7 senior Oral Communications classes at Sagami Women's University High School, who acted as the official guinea pigs and suffered through a lot of corrections. Also thanks to the debate team at International Christian University, particularly Kazue Tani, who got me out of debate retirement and set into motion the wheels that made this text possible.

Published by Tuttle Publishing, an imprint of Periplus Editions (HK) Ltd., with editorial offices at 364 Innovation Drive, North Clarendon, Vermont 05759 and 130 Joo Seng Road, #06-01-03, Singapore 368357.

© 1999 Periplus Editions (HK) Ltd.
All rights reserved. No part of this publication may be reproduced or transmitted in any form or by any means, electronic or mechanical, including photocopying, recording, or any information storage and retrieval system, without permission in writing from the publisher.

First Tuttle edition, 1999
ISBN 0-8048-3656-6
ISBN 4-8053-0782-X (for sale in Japan only)

Distributors

Japan: Tuttle Publishing, Yaekari Bldg 3F, 5-4-12 Osaki, Shinagawa-ku, Tokyo 141-0032.
Tel: (03) 5437 0171; Fax: (03) 5437 0755; Email: tuttle-sales@gol.com
North America, Latin America & Europe: Tuttle Publishing, 364 Innovation Drive, North Clarendon, VT 05759-9436, USA. Tel: (802) 773 8930; Fax: (802) 773 6993; Email: info@tuttlepublishing.com; Website: www.tuttlepublishing.com
Asia-Pacific: Berkeley Books Pte. Ltd., 130 Joo Seng Road #06-01/03 Singapore 368357.
Tel: (65) 6280 1330; Fax: (65) 6280 6290; Email: inquiries@periplus.com.sg; Website: www.periplus.com
Indonesia: PT. Java Books Indonesia, Jl. Kelapa Gading Kirana, Blok A14 No.17, Jakarta 14240, Indonesia.
Tel: (62-21) 451 5351; Fax: (62-21) 453 4987; Email: cs@javabooks.co.id

08 07 06 05   6 5 4 3

Printed in Singapore

TUTTLE PUBLISHING® is a registered trademark of Tuttle Publishing.